W9-ABY-269

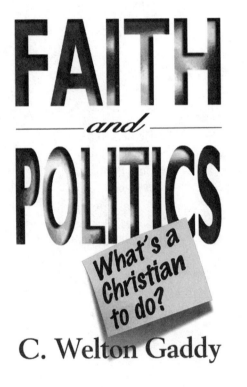

FAITH
and
POLITICS

What's a Christian to do?

C. Welton Gaddy

Dedicated to
Brooks Hays
"Model Politician"
(*in memoriam*)
and
Henlee H. Barnette
"Instructor in Life"

FAITH

—— *and* ——

POLITICS

What's a Christian to Do?

C. Welton Gaddy

PEAKE ROAD

Macon, Georgia

ISBN 1-57312-046-4

Faith and Politics
What's a Christian to Do?

C. Welton Gaddy

6316 Peake Road
Macon, Georgia 31210-3960
1-800-747-3016

Peake Road
is an imprint of
Smyth & Helwys Publishing, Inc.®

Library of Congress #96-11296

Contents

Preface

Personal faith seeks social expression. No area of life is exempt from faith's concern. Private affirmations of faith inspire public actions that bear witness to the values and priorities of the faith affirmed. Often the social demands of faith are clear, and the path of obedience to faith readily understandable even if difficult. But not in the political realm.

Politics present a peculiar challenge to faith, especially politics within a democratic form of government. Faith prizes certainty and finds compromise repugnant. Politics trade in ambiguity, and value compromise as essential to decision-making. Desiring for everyone to embrace the same religion, faith engages in evangelism. Politics appreciate diversity and protect every person's right to be different. Faith lauds freedom as the environment most desirable for a healthy practice of religion. Politics praise freedom as a condition under which people can choose against religion as well as for it.

When conscientious expressions of faith encounter the complex challenges of politics, questions arise: Does my faith demand support for a particular form of government and require opposition to all other forms? Or, is government the one realm of life that should be off-limits to faith? How can I maintain enthusiastic certainty about my religious convictions and support a government-guaranteed freedom that allows other persons to argue against and even outright reject my religious point of view? Should I seek enforcement of my moral values within society by means of government legislation? If not, why not? Are politics and religion always on a crash course in relation to each other?

On the pages that follow, I attempt to answer some of the more troubling questions about politics and religion that presently nag at the public's social conscience. Not that my answers will silence these questions; they won't. My words are sure to evoke new inquiries or fire the passion with which people re-ask old ones. But at least a few affirmations for examination will be on the table alongside steadily mounting stacks of weighty questions.

I write as a Christian, although the methods of interaction between government and religion that I suggest and the directions for their cooperation to which I point apply to people of other faiths as well. My responses to pressing questions about politics and faith have taken form at the intersection where biblical studies, political analysis, theological convictions, and personal experiences meet.

The material in this book is not inconsequential nationally or personally. To be sure, the text I have written does not contain the only words of truth or the last word on truth regarding the subjects discussed. However, this little volume affirms a few basic principles that, I believe, can withstand the rigors of national examination, bring a measure of clarification to the terrible confusion that currently shrouds discussions of politics and religion, and make a contribution to the political thoughts and actions that stem from people's religious convictions.

Acknowledgments

Seldom, if ever, is a book the product of one person alone. This one certainly isn't. I have benefited from the research and insights of countless numbers of people whose names do not appear anywhere in this little volume. Though I have tried to credit each source of information, I apologize to any who have not been properly recognized.

Joseph Conn, editor of *Church & State* magazine, and John Paul Gaddy, a high school civics teacher, have checked the manuscript for substantive errors. Any errors that remain are my responsibility, however, not theirs.

Scott Nash of Smyth & Helwys Publishers encouraged this project from the time of our first discussion about it. When it became a title under the imprint of Peake Road, David Cassady and Jackie Riley offered good counsel and practiced amazing patience in editing the manuscript.

My wife Judy has understood, granted, and protected the stretches of silence needed for reading, thinking, and writing.

Northminster Church in Monroe, Louisiana, continues to encourage my interest in writing and views an endeavor like this one as, at least in part, an extension of our corporate ministry.

To all who have assisted and encouraged, thanks.

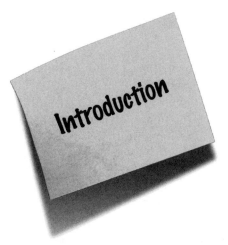

Introduction

Questions, questions, questions! Presently questions encircle the political landscape in the United States like flag poles surround the Washington Monument in our nation's capital. Inject faith into discussions of politics, and a dense fog seems to descend upon the whole scene. Achieving clarity in vision ranges from difficult to impossible.

A National Dilemma

It's anybody's guess whether faith or politics generates the most excitement today. My bet is on politics. Combine the two concerns, though, and heated dialogues, fiery debates, or maybe even explosive conflicts develop. Virtually everyone holds a strong opinion about politics and faith. Seldom, however, are two people's thoughts exactly alike. Subsequently, a confident declaration about faith and politics by one person generates probing questions on that subject from another person.

This inquiries-littered pattern of interpersonal reactions to the relationship between faith and politics has an institutional counterpart. Right now, government agencies seriously question the role of religious organizations in the political process. Several religious entities have violated their promise of a non-political mission and lost their tax-exempt status. Reciprocally, churches, temples, and mosques query government bodies about their processes of decision-making as well as challenge the morality of many of their policies. Concerned onlookers watch this back-and-forth exchange of questions with dismay and want to know why governmental and religious institutions devote so much time and attention to each other.

Embittered debates about morals and politics dominate news media. Candidates for public office carefully try to appease the aggressive political action arms of various religious bodies without scaring off more religiously passive advocates of an opposing persuasion. Litigation initiated by religious liberty issues increases. The Supreme Court judiciously redefines the line of demarcation between civil governments and religious organizations. The President of the United States tries to clarify historic provisions of the First Amendment within an emotionally charged context of religious fervor and anti-religious hostility. Congress fearlessly plays politics with constitutional amendments that jeopardize the free exercise of religion. Every election at every level of government—from local school board issues to a national campaign for the presidency—is a battleground on which forces of good and evil duke it out.

I appreciate questions and enjoy raising them. As conventional wisdom asserts, however, even too much of a good thing can go bad. At some point, a few solid answers to troubling inquiries must emerge to make grappling with more questions tolerable. Not just any answers will do, though. Every bit as dangerous as too many questions are absolutist assertions thrown down as gauntlets to silence healthy debate. People who brandish a definitive response for every inquiry and defensively recognize no shadow of doubt or possibility of viable disagreement with their positions seriously threaten the democratic process.

It's an ironic situation. Personal opinions, organizational decrees, and party platforms related to the relationship between faith and politics abound. Yet, the nation suffers from a lack of thoughtful responses to fundamental inquiries. Part of the problem resides in the avalanche of declared viewpoints that has edged its way across our country. This onslought of smothering certainty has silenced the questions that most need to be asked, questions that invite answers that revitalize the body politic and nurture its health. Asking the right questions is more than half the battle in finding helpful answers to dangerous situations.

Structure of the Book

On the pages that follow, you will encounter the moral-political questions that trouble me most. That's either because other people regularly request that I respond to these questions or because, in my own mind, I have not been able to resolve the conflict to which they point.

Here's the plan of the book. I have compiled four sets of questions intended to facilitate an examination of the relationship between faith and politics generally, study specific political platform issues from a moral perspective, evaluate the most important qualifications of a candidate for an elected office, and ponder the kind of political vision that seems most consistent with the Christian faith. Each division of the book contains three different kinds of material.

Personal Pilgrimage. My own pilgrimage related to faith and politics forms the background out of which the questions to be dealt with have arisen. That personal journey also provides the backdrop against which suggested answers to these inquiries take shape.

Fundamental Inquiries. I have attempted to listen carefully to conversations repeated daily in offices, hair salons, restaurants, churches, and civic organizations in virtually every community across our nation. On the basis of what I have overheard, I have listed the most impassioned questions frequently asked about the role of religion in our national life. These inquiries constitute the skeleton around which the content of the book is fleshed out.

Basic Principles. My responses to the fundamental inquiries in this volume draw from a wide spectrum of sources. I address specific political-religious dilemmas with the help of materials based upon speeches and writings of major players currently active on a national stage, basic moral theories, theological doctrines, biblical literature, personal experience, and the Constitution of the United States.

Vision and Hope

A dominant vision challenges and informs every word I write. I see honest individuals struggling to make enough sense of the contemporary political situation and the demands of their faith (What's a

Christian to do?) to function as responsible citizens (bringing their religious faith to bear on political questions and actions). The people I envision contribute to the general welfare of the nation while honoring their spiritual, moral, and political convictions. These people do not agree with each other, however. Consensus opinions do not develop even among individuals who construct their political views on the foundation of the same religious faith.

I write harboring no illusion of settling the debates that swirl around the questions to which I respond. My intention is to inform these discussions as I encourage their continuation. Likewise, I have no desire to define what people ought to think or to prescribe precisely how people ought to bring faith to bear on politics. However, I sincerely hope to identify a few basic principles that can enable individuals to express their religious faith in the political arena in a manner supportive of freedom and faithful to historic Christian convictions.

Part I

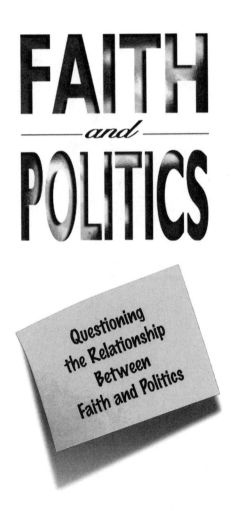

FAITH
and
POLITICS

Questioning
the Relationship
Between
Faith and Politics

Notes from a Personal Pilgrimage

"Religion and politics don't mix!" That long-standing, widely-influential myth represented conventional wisdom when I wrote my first article on Christianity and politics. Advocating Christians' involvement in the political process was not easy toward the conclusion of the turbulent decade of "the '60s."

The civil rights movement and the nation's military involvement in Southeast Asia left Christians, like the rest of society, deeply divided. A few Christian denominations actively supported the campaign for civil rights and opposed the war in Vietnam. In response, other Christians hardened their conviction about the inappropriateness of a religious presence in the political arena.

I had heard the old "religion and politics don't mix" cliché for most of my life, often from respected friends. The statement never had rung true for me, however. A serious study of the Bible, which my home church commended to me as the divinely-inspired basis for belief and behavior, led me to conclusions about Christians' political responsibilities that differed dramatically from prevailing thought in the congregation of my childhood and youth.

Working for Change

In 1971, I accepted an invitation to join the staff of the Christian Life Commission of the Southern Baptist Convention. My specific assignment in the social ethics agency of my denomination was Christian citizenship development. The executive of the commission, Foy Valentine, challenged me to inspire and mobilize Christians in our denomination to become responsibly informed about government and actively involved in politics while maintaining the historic principle of church-state separation.

I hesitantly left a fulfilling pastorate to do this new work. I knew that Christians had the potential to make significant positive contributions to government. I was also very much aware that, as a group, Christians remained deathly silent and conspicuously absent in most political conversations. My new job consistently challenged me and periodically threatened to overwhelm me. I knew it was right for Southern Baptists, for the times, and for me.

Early in the decade of the 1970s, only a few mainline denominations even attempted to exert political influence on the national scene.

Almost without exception, conservative Christians—the believers I knew best—viewed political action with suspicion and considered government an arena outside the parameters of biblically-based evangelism.

In 1965, Jerry Falwell had told his parishioners at the Thomas Road Baptist Church in Lynchburg, Virginia:

> Nowhere are we commissioned to reform the externals. . . . Believing the Bible as I do, I would find it impossible to stop preaching the pure saving gospel of Jesus Christ, and begin . . . fighting communism or participating in civil rights reforms.[1]

Similarly, at that time, Pat Robertson viewed political involvement on the part of Christians with extreme disfavor, speaking of political power's ability to corrupt all it touched. Robertson abstained from his father's 1966 campaign for re-election to the United States Senate and expressed gratitude when his father lost that election. "My father's defeat was of the Lord, for his soul was far more important than his seniority in Washington," Robertson explained.[2]

Convinced that responsible citizenship in one's nation is an essential characteristic of faithful discipleship under God's reign, I went about my work in Christian citizenship development with a sense of urgency, enthusiasm, and divine calling. Soon, though, I began to question the wisdom of my mission.

Witnessing a Revolution

In the mid-1970s, scores of conservative Christians reversed their opinion about keeping politics and religion separated. Suddenly, many believers who had thoughtlessly disdained government, with equal thoughtlessness, embraced political action as their primary evangelistic endeavor. They began to speak of government as a major means of "Christianizing" America.

I looked and listened with dismay as a growing number of individuals wed the very terms to which I devoted so much attention— "responsible political participation," "Christian citizenship," and "moral involvement in the government"—to the right-wing political agenda of fundamentalist religionists. Nothing wrong with that, but the new religious-political activists were interested in control rather than influence. They tied the language of responsible Christian citizenship exclusively to goals of political involvement, methods of political action, and principles of church-state relations that I found morally irresponsible, at best, and, at worst, theologically reprehensible.

A lack of political sophistication did little to lessen the fervor of religious conservatives or slow down their political activities. Having found a new mission field, these freshly-energized people of God would not rest until they had canvased the land, buttonholing citizens with their message about "Christian politics." Almost over night, it seemed, passionate protests against political involvement gave way to enthusiastic endorsements of politics as a medium for Christian ministry—the latter with no more theological discretion than the former.

What a shift! A sea change! A revolution! In a relatively short period of time, a sizable segment of the Christian community in the United States completely reversed its position on political involvement. In light moments, I laughingly claimed great success for my efforts to get Christians involved in the political process. At more somber moments, though, the thoughtless plunge into politics on the part of many in the Christian community made me feel like a complete failure. My own role in this whole matter was minimal, but I was rightly positioned to have maximum reasons for concern.

My concern about faith and politics, religion and government, persists. Persons who long abstained from politics now immerse themselves in political action as a primal expression of their Christian convictions. Within my own denomination, many ministers now set aside a longstanding tradition of professional silence on partisan political issues and personalities to endorse (or condemn) both candidates and issues-positions via church stationary emanating from their offices and sermons preached from their pulpits. It is a new day for Christians and politics, but the dangers of the present are as grave as those created by Christians' complete absence from politics in another day.

Questioning Everything

Many people view churches' espousal of moral responsibility and engagement in political activities with bewilderment, if not outright confusion. Have Christian congregations been politicized? Or, have churches baptized politics? Clear distinctions no longer separate the religious agenda from the political agenda of many religious leaders. That bothers me and raises all kinds of questions in my mind.

Still somewhat dazed by the alarming speed with which religious organizations have become politicized, I find myself wondering about my basic convictions on Christian citizenship. Do my thoughts suffer from a major flaw? How can truths that I hold dear be used to justify actions completely antithetical to my beliefs about politics, freedom, and Christian discipleship? Sometimes I am even tempted to endorse again the old axiom that "politics and religion don't mix." But, I can't do that.

I suspect an increasingly dangerous confusion between religious and political movements jeopardizes the health of our nation and threatens to compromise the integrity of the Christian faith. Conscientious persons cannot leave this situation unexamined. Still convinced of the importance of faith finding political expression, though seriously concerned about abuses to both religion and politics carried out under the banner of "Christian citizenship," I feel compelled to restudy old convictions and to raise new questions about the relationship between faith and politics. I need a fresh appraisal of the relationship between Christian discipleship and civil citizenship in my own spiritual pilgrimage. Perhaps my work can prove beneficial to others also.

What brought about the present confusion regarding the relationship between faith and politics? Is there a way out of the mess we're in?

During the darkest days of our nation's military involvement in Southeast Asia, several mainline Christian denominations sought to exert political influence aimed at ending that conflict. Convinced of the immorality of the war in Vietnam, church-based lobbyists charged Capitol Hill with a political vigor seldom before seen among religious people. The war was an ethical issue, and the church knew ethics.

Simultaneously, religiously-oriented political activists threw their support behind social legislation considered crucial to the moral health of the nation. And, they succeeded. Neither the Johnson Administration's "war on poverty," passage of groundbreaking civil rights legislation, nor the cessation of the war in Vietnam can be understood adequately apart from the political muscle flexed by Christian political organizations.

Conservative Christians remained mostly absent from the religious community's efforts to stop the war in Southeast Asia and guarantee justice through new domestic initiatives. Silence from this segment of Christianity soon gave way to boisterous activity, however. Disfavor with the presidency of Jimmy Carter stoked fires of political enthusiasm among conservative Christians. On the eve of the 1980s, looking to expand their power base in the nation, many major conservative religious organizations linked up with conservative political forces—primarily Republicans disenchanted with their party's shift toward a moderate posture. The New Right emerged as a formidable factor in American politics.

National Religious Right organizations proliferated. Jerry Falwell launched the Moral Majority. Ed McAteer developed the Religious Roundtable. Robert Grant and Richard Zone co-founded the Christian Voice. Robert Billings formed the National Christian Action Coalition. These newly conceived structures for giving political influence to conservataive Christians worked in cooperation with the National Conservative Political Action Committee organized by Terry Dolan, the Conservative Caucus formed by Howard Phillips, and the Committee for the Survival of a Free Congress and the Heritage Foundation founded by Paul Weyrich. All these organizations benefited immensely from the direct mail wizardry of Richard Viguerie who had collected twenty to thirty million names for a publicity and fund-raising campaign.

Winning the Presidency

During the 1980 presidential campaign, New Right religious organizations achieved an unprecedented zenith of political power and influence. Jerry Falwell pronounced the invocation at the Republicans' national convention. Eight weeks later, Ronald Reagan, the Republican nominee for the presidency of the United States, appeared on the program of the Religious Roundtable's National Affairs Briefing and enthusiastically commended the political work of the Religious Right.

Confusion developed. Self-declared "religious" organizations vigorously worked to defeat the only candidate for the presidency who openly articulated Christian convictions. Conservative Christians amassed monumental support for a presidential candidate whose religious background appeared ambiguous at best. Onlookers scratched their heads and asked, "What does it mean to be a Christian? Is Christianity defined by political convictions or spiritual commitments?"

Voter registration campaigns, often based in local churches, targeted Christian fundamentalists who had not previously voted in national elections. Organizations such as the Christian Voice distributed "moral report cards" that rated the performance of members of the United States Congress according to their votes on issues of importance to the Religious Right. More and more the public suspected that a rather narrow political agenda, not historic Christian faith, served as the primary criterion by which members of the Religious Right determined which candidates for public office to support.

The political power-surge of New Right religious organizations paid off in the national election of 1980. Pollsters attributed at least two-thirds of Ronald Reagan's margin of victory in the presidential election to white fundamentalist voters. Of the twenty-eight Congress persons whom evangelical groups targeted for defeat in this election, twenty-three lost their seats on Capitol Hill. Jerry Falwell called this national election day, "The greatest day for the cause of conservatism and American morality in my adult life."[3]

Evangelical Christians seemed to be on an unstoppable roll. Confusion between religious action and political action worsened. Then, suddenly the confusion subsided. Surprisingly, the New Right movement among religionists fizzled out. By the advent of the 1980s, most of the Religious Right organizations formed in the late 1970s had disbanded.

After his defeat in the 1988 presidential race, Pat Robertson decided to draw upon the campaign structures he had in place and to utilize his impressive mailing list to form a new religious organization with a political agenda. Subsequently, Robertson established the Christian Coalition to "mobilize and train Christians for effective political action." In the spring of 1990, Ralph Reed, whom Robertson chose to lead the Christian Coalition, pinpointed the mission of this new movement: "What Christians have got to do is take back this country, one precinct at a time, one neighborhood at a time, and one state at a time."[4]

Several new Religious Right organizations quickly formed in the wake of Robertson's initiative. Each tended to be more politically sophisticated and better financed than their predecessors.

The Epitome of Confusion

Shortly after the national conventions of the two major political parties in 1992, on August 22 at the Dallas (Texas) Convention Center, a prominent Republican charged that the platform of the Democratic Party had "left out three simple letters: G-O-D." Conversely, the Republicans' political platform contained a specific reference to Deity. Spokespersons for the Republican Party later explained that their party wanted to honor God by placing God's name in their platform. (Don't you know God was relieved!)

But did the Republicans' platform committee have to vote on whether or not God's name should be included? And were the provisions in this platform worthy of God's name being attached to it? Did inserting "G-O-D" into that document make it a more religious document than the statement that came from the Democrats' platform committee?

This situation, like no other, epitomized the mounting confusion regarding proper relationships between Christians, Christianity, and politics. God will not be co-opted as the mascot for any political group. Using the divine name to gain votes does not honor God.

The present state of confusion is unfortunate, and to a great degree unnecessary. However, the current morass prompts a question that points toward a way out of the confusion: How *is* God honored in the political process? Answering that inquiry conscientiously mandates a careful examination of the teachings of the Bible.

What does the Bible say about a Christian's role in politics?

No part of the Bible was written under a form of government even similar to that of the United States. Each section of the Scriptures reflects the historical context and political environment in which it was written. For that reason, the Bible contains several different estimates of the nature of government and the role of God's people in politics.

Old Testament Background

Early Israelites understood citizenship more in terms of biological descent than shared life in a commonly-administerd geographical area. Individuals claimed an Israelite identity not because of where they lived but because of the family into which they were born. Governance among nomadic Israelites took on the look of a primitive form of democracy. All adult males constituted a body known as "the assembly" or "the congregation" (Num 26:2), which acted with authority in the life of the nation. Seniority and experience elevated persons to the status of "elders" in this governing body. The assembly functioned mostly as a deliberative body. Responsibility for the development and enforcement of laws and other government policies fell the lot of a high leader and those to whom he delegated authority. The assembly retained the right to depose the person in this position and to reelect another, however.

The idea of a covenant dominated the corporate life of Israel. Moses had guided the people into a covenant relationship with God. When the tribes of Israel and various groups of Israelites eventually settled down, this covenant alone brought unity out of their vast diversity.

Later, after 200 years of autonomous tribal life, the people of Israel recognized their need for a more centralized government. No dominant leader with the charismatic attractiveness and stabilizing power of Moses had appeared during this long stretch of time. Responding to what various individuals believed to be a directive from God, Israel anointed a king. Local government under a monarch differed little from the style of rule found in the high leader, but in both a sense of God's guidance prevailed.

New Testament View

At least three different perspectives on government appear in the primitive Christian community of faith. Each dictated a variation in the way individual Christians were expected to relate to the state.

Paul offered glowing generalizations about the goodness of government and encouraged Christians to prayerfully support government leaders. The man from Tarsus viewed government as a provision from

God that held in check the selfishness of humankind and promoted the social good. Writing to Christians in Rome, Paul announced that the authorities were ministers of God (Rom 13:1-7). He commended government as a beneficial social institution willed by God, though not divine in itself, to which the people of God should be submissive. Resistance to the government could be justified only when the will of the government clashed with obedience to God. Even then, though, resisting Christians were morally obligated to pray for the authorities.

Paul framed his remarks about government as a proud citizen of Rome. The missionary apostle recognized that the invaluable contributions of Roman authorities to society—a commitment to justice, a durable peace, and excellent routes for transportation—greatly benefited the spread of Christianity. Naturally, Paul saw no reason for opposition to Roman rule. He considered support for the government a moral responsibility.

Government as a Horrible Evil

Not everyone in the New Testament world shared Paul's positive experience of government. Take the author of Revelation for example—a man named John who, from the site of his captivity on the Island of Patmos, penned words of encouragement to Christians suffering under the persecution of a demented Roman ruler. John viewed government quite differently from his predecessor in the faith named Paul. Surrounded by the persecution of followers of Christ who refused to burn incense to the "godhead" of Caesar, John described government as "a beast" (Rev 13:1-8).

Keep in mind that the government John described as a beast in competition with God was the same government earlier praised by Paul as an instrument of God. Only the leaders of that government had changed. Healthy respect for the emperor had escalated (or degenerated) into a diabolical form of emperor worship.

Good institutions can go bad. Even political movements willed by God sometimes fall into the hands of evil persons and lose their value. Even so, John encouraged his readers to obey the legitimate demands of government leaders (Rev 13:10) and offered no incentive for rebellion. Persecuted Christians of this era continued to pray for the very government leaders who inflicted pain on them (1 Tim 2:1-3).

Government and God

Jesus' words about civil government reflect neither the negativism of John nor the positivism of Paul. Jesus recognized government as a legitimate social institution with a right to level certain demands for support upon its citizens (payment of taxes, for example). He encouraged his followers to live in submission to civil authorities.

Jesus viewed government as a temporary institution possessing only limited power, however. He warned his followers against assigning equal importance to the reign of a government official and the leadership of God. "Give therefore to the emperor the things that are the emperor's, and to God the things that are God's" (Matt 22:21), Jesus advised. According to the teachings of Jesus, obedience to the government must always be secondary to allegiance to God, but fidelity to the leadership of God results in civil actions.

When Jesus spoke, giving the government its due meant little more than obeying laws and paying taxes. The emperor's rule made no provision for any other form of involvement on the part of Christians. Set in the context of a democracy, however, Jesus' instructions prompt a much wider range of actions. Giving to a democratic form of government what belongs to it involves active personal participation in political processes, informed voting, regular communication with government officials, and maybe even running for an elected office.

Basic Principles of Bible-Based Citizenship

Despite variables in the different perspectives on government represented in the Bible, a few basic principles regarding a person's relationship to the state remained constant throughout the Scriptures.

(1) Demonstrate a respect for government leaders that transcends the specific individuals who occupy an office at any given time. Respect does not demand blind allegiance and differs immeasurably from worship.

(2) Pray for government officials regardless of their moral character. A government leader is never too evil to not merit the prayers of God's people.

(3) Submit to civil authorities unless obedience to rulers compromises faithfulness to God. If fidelity to God results in punishment from the government, so be it. Bear the consequences of absolute devotion to God as a mark of honest spirituality.

(4) Resist the government when it demands more than its due; resist but refuse to rebel. A decision in favor of disobedient resistance requires an acceptance of the consequences of such behavior.

(5) Live out discipleship in the civil arena as in every other area of life. Seek to follow the will of God in political action as well as in spiritual decision-making.

These five principles derive from specific biblical texts that address the subject of government. But there's more. Some of the most important guidelines for Christians' relations to government appear in scripture passages that do not even mention the words "government," "politics," or "citizenship."

Jesus admonished his disciples to live in the world as "salt," "light," and "leaven." Within a democracy, compliance with Christ's metaphors of change through penetration thrusts Christians into the political sphere. Involvement in government becomes a major medium for establishing justice, guaranteeing equality, and responding to social needs.

Similarly, the apostle Paul admonished Christians to live in a manner worthy of the gospel. Paul chose to express the inclusive nature of his thought through the word from which we derive the term "politics." In other words, the apostle wrote, "Let your politics be worthy of the gospel of Christ." We can serve God through our activities in the halls of government as well as in a church.

Christians and politicians are not antithetical concepts. An individual can be both a Christian and a politician. In fact, God wills as much for all of us.

What is a "Christian politician"?
How do you identify one?

On a radio news program in Dallas, Texas, in 1980, I asked a member of the Religious Roundtable to specify the reasons he supported Ronald Reagan and opposed Jimmy Carter for the presidency of the

United States. The man explained that Reagan's policy positions were more "Christian" than Carter's. When I pressed for a specific illustration of one candidate's moral superiority to the other on a platform issue, the man across the table from me pointed to Reagan's opposition to the Panama Canal Treaty, which Carter supported. Then, the Reagan supporter praised his candidate's stance as "the New Testament position."

Such a cut-and-dried spiritual approach to political loyalties baffles me. Besides, what does the New Testament say about the Panamal Canal Treaty? The rationale for joining partisan political campaigns under the guise of support for biblical principles escapes me. Of course, scriptural truth is at stake in many political issues. But to claim loyalty to the Bible as a justification for endorsing purely political decisions misrepresents the nature of Christianity and jeopardizes healthy political debate. A few basic definitions can enlighten this kind of conversation considerably.

Who Is a "Politician"?

A politician is a person involved in politics, and politics is the art of government. Though we tend to use the term "politics" almost exclusively in relation to civil government, politics exist in all social institutions—from families to corporations, from churches to legislatures. By means of politics, people seek to build broad-based acceptance for their ideas about how a society best functions (laws, finances, infrastructures, and so on). A politician is a person who exerts political influence and engages in political action.

Who Is a "Christian"?

A Christian is a person who pledges love, loyalty, and life to Jesus Christ. A Christian follows Jesus, acknowledging him as the Son of God, the Messiah, the Savior of the world, and the Lord of life.

No political litmus test provides a fool-proof method for establishing the authenticity of a person's Christianity. That's just as well. Jesus warned his followers to refrain from passing judgment on each other. God alone has the ultimate insight into the reality of an individual's Christian identity.

Political loyalties aside, when it comes to recognizing an individual as a Christian, we are left to respect that person's confession of beliefs and demonstration of spiritual discipleship. Political disagreements do not justify judgmental attacks on a person's spiritual condition.

Who Is a Christian Politican?

A Christian politician is a follower of Jesus Christ who is involved in the politics of government. That's it. Of course, that's enough. But, there is no more to the definition. And, there can be no less. An individual who professes Jesus Christ as Lord and seeks to live out that conviction within the realm of political action is a Christian politician.

Congressional scorecards that report an individual's voting record on various pieces of important legislation can profile that person's political posture. Similarly, voter guides that highlight the planks in an individual's political platform provide helpful insights into a candidate's political priorities. Neither a political platform nor a voting record can determine a politician's Christian identity, however. That determination rests solely upon an individual's relationship with God as revealed in Jesus Christ.

While I was working in Washington, D.C., for Southern Baptists, I got to know Senators Mark Hatfield and George McGovern very well. These two men sat on opposite sides of the aisle in the chamber of the United States Senate. Hatfield was a Republican, and McGovern a Democrat. Each supported legislative proposals and candidates for public offices that the other opposed. Both, though, were accomplished politicians and unabashedly loyal followers of Jesus Christ —two of the most devout persons I have ever met.

The Christian devotion of Mark Hatfield and George McGovern was a matter of record for all who knew them. The substance of their Christianity could not be determined by their political affiliations and legislative actions. Like many others who serve on Capitol Hill, these two individuals knew how to disagree with colleagues politically without questioning the sincerity of their opponents' faith commitments.

Identifying a Christian politician requires a consideration of an individual's confessed belief concerning the lordship of Jesus Christ, not a measurement of that person's loyalty to a political party, issue, or strategy. Presently, a barrage of charges and countercharges regarding Christianity, morality, and politics threatens to displace biblical truth with political bias. When talking and writing about Christian politicians, the least we can do is insist on accurate definitions of the two terms that make up that identity.

Exactly what is the Religious Right?
What's wrong with its political agenda?

"Religious Right" is the name given to politically and theologically conservative religious groups actively involved in politics to oppose pluralism and church-state separation and to promote the establishment of their religious and moral points of view. Most members of the Religious Right are Protestants, although a small number of anti-church-state-separation Orthodox Jews and a few extremely traditional Catholics identify with the movement.

The Religious Right stands at the epicenter of a nation-quake too strong for measurement on the Richter scale. A frightening shift of values threatens to reorder completely the relationship between faith and politics. The movement is shaking the foundations of fundamental rights guaranteed by the United States Constitution.

Though Religious Right supporters are generally conservative, not all conservatives support this religious-political phenomenon. Many conservatives in our society actually oppose the agenda of the Religious Right.

Major Players in the Religous Right
Individuals and Organizations

The Religious Right can be better understood by identifying some of the specific people and organizations of prominence in the movement. Here is a sampling:

Pat Robertson and the Christian Coalition. Pat Robertson presently wears the mantel of leadership in the Religious Right. After his failed bid for the presidency of the nation in 1988, Robertson turned his attention to grass-roots political education and organization. From his host's chair on the nationally televised program called the "700 Club," Robertson spins political prophecies, evaluates personalities, and endorses issues using the language and demeanor of conservative Christianity. Viewers who tune into Robertson's video "ministry" for spiritual enrichment get a full dose of political indoctrination through Robertson's biblical analysis of the news and "words of knowledge" received from God. Robertson has amassed an amazing power base and accumulated incredible wealth. He owns the Christian Broadcasting Network (valued at $1,000,000,000), the Family Channel on cable television (valued at $90,000,000), a fax-based news service known as Zap News, a four-diamond hotel, the Ice Capades, syndication rights to several popular television programs, and diamond mines in Central Africa. From such a position of power, Robertson has founded Regent University, the American Center for Law and Justice, and the Christian Coalition.

Robertson announces the will of God and declares political wisdom with a confidence and smugness that make me uncomfortable. For example, he claims his Regent Law School trains students in "God's perspective on the law." Whose God? Or, whose perspective on God? How does he know? Robertson asserts that the United States Constitution makes no provision for church-state separation, which he considers a lie blocking the way to godly government. How did Madison and Jefferson, who helped write the document, get it so wrong? And, why has church-state separation served both religion and the nation so well for all these years?

Pat Robertson launched the Christian Coalition in 1988 "to mobilize and train Christians for effective political action." Subsequently, he chose an energetic young man named Ralph Reed to handle the day-to-day operations of the organization as its executive director.

Claiming 1.6 million members, the Christian Coalition has forged a strong bond with the Republican Party. According to most political analysts, the Christian Coalition exercises a dominant influence in 18 states' Republican parties and a substantial influence in the Republican parties of 13 other states. Republican Speaker of the House of Representatives, Newt Gingrich, credited the Christian Coalition with his party's victories in the 1994 elections. After all, the Coalition had spent more than $1,000,000 building national support for Newt Gingrich's "Contract with America." In May 1995, the Christian Coalition announced a contract of its own: "Contract with the American Family." Republican leaders rushed to endorse this ten-point, wide-ranging program that advocates among other initiatives the following:

- a voucher system that allows the use of federal funds in support of private education
- a constitutional amendment to allow prayer at public events
- the abolishment of the Department of Education with a subsequent transfer of all funding for education to local school boards and families
- privatizing the arts by eliminating all funding for groups such as the National Endowment for the Arts and Humanities, the Corporation for Public Broadcasting, and the Legal Services Corporation
- limits on late term abortions, a repeal of requirements that Medicaid funds be used to pay for abortions, and the termination of federal funds for organizations that provide abortion counseling or perform abortions.

Though the Christian Coalition works closely with more than thirty other organizations, not all conservative Christians support it. Some conservative Christians fear the coalition's close alignment with the Republican Party, charging that cosolidating Republican political control has become more important to the coalition than advancing its social agenda. Two popular conservative theologians, Tony Campolo and Jim Wallis, drafted a statement endorsed by more than 100 other national religious leaders challenging the Religious Right. According to Wallis and Campolo,

> The moral authority necessary to mitigate the excesses of power has been replaced by a thirst for political influence. The almost total identification of the Religious Right with the new Republican majority in Washington is a dangerous liaison of religion with political power.[5]

James Dobson and Focus on the Family. Another major personality has stepped to the forefront of the Religious Right movement. For many years the name of James Dobson was virtually synonymous with an emphasis on and support for the Christian family. Through his books, radio shows, movies, and conferences, Dobson helpfully addressed the many dynamics with which a family must cope successfully in order to stay together. Dobson's ministry known as Focus on the Family helped literally thousands of people.

Recently, James Dobson has begun using the mailing list comprised of the names of people who have responded to Focus on the Family to promote his personal political platform. Dobson exercises great influence in the lives of individuals open to his every suggestion and vulnerable to manipulation because of the help they previously received from him. A former Justice Department lawyer, now heavily involved in the Religious Right, observed, "James Dobson is the heavy hitter in the conservative Christian movement. He commands armies of people."[6]

Dobson stays in touch with his followers. In addition to his 10 radio shows, 11 magazines, books, and videos, Dobson produces curriculum guides for churches, fillers for church bulletins, and a monthly letter that goes to 2.1 million people. Each week he faxes suggested sermon topics and materials to thousands of pastors. Staff workers on Capitol Hill say they can always tell when Dobson has called his people to action because their fax machines and e-mail equipment work overtime.

Predictably, when Dobson speaks, many politicians listen. In March 1995, via a radio broadcast, Dobson warned the Republican Party that it was taking a "precarious path" by focusing too narrowly on fiscal issues. In a letter to 2,000,000 of his supporters, Dobson threatened to abandon the Republican Party if its leaders halted their anti-abortion campaign. Dobson reminded Republicans that losing only 5 percent of the nation's evangelical Christian voters could prove fatal to their election efforts in 1996.

And a Whole Host of Others. The advent of Pat Robertson's Christian Coalition in 1988 marked the beginning of a virtual explosion of new Religious Right organizations across the United States. Each has a niche in the movement, a cadre of supporters, and a realm of influence. Only a partial listing of the organizations and their leaders indicates the size and power of this religio-political campaign.

As the legal arm of the Christian Coalition, Pat Robertson brought into existence The American Center for Law and Justice in 1990. Viewed as an American Civil Liberties Union for Christians, this organization takes on high-profile legal cases related to anti-abortion activities and the free exercise of religion in schools. However, church-state separationists fault the ACLJ for trying to interject sectarianism into public schools, not protecting the right of a free exercise of religion. The law center is ably led by Jay Sekulow, its chief counsel, and Keith Fournier, its executive director.

Donald Wildmon founded The American Family Association in 1987 (the successor to The National Federation for Decency) to promote "the biblical ethic of decency in American society," giving primary attention to television and other media. Wildmon also created the American Family Association Law Center in 1989 to support prayer in public schools and to launch an attack on certain curricula in public schools. Peggy Coleman serves as the legal counsel for Wildmon's law center.

Aiming to protect the rights of the family through prayer and action, Beverly LaHaye founded Concerned Women for America in 1979. LaHaye views her organization as the alternative to the National Organization for Women. She works in close cooperation with Pat Robertson's American Center for Law and Justice.

In 1983, Louis P. Sheldon founded the Traditional Values Coalition to battle homosexuality, which he views as "the most pernicious evil today." Sheldon also brought into existence the Traditional Values Lobby, which works among educators; the American Liberties Institute, a research organization focusing on biblical concepts in the founding of the nation and the writing of the Constitution; the California Business for Traditional Values; and the National Task Force for the Preservation of the Heterosexual Ethic in America.

Also in 1983, in an effort to turn public schools toward favoritism for the Christian faith, Robert L. Simonds founded Citizens for Excellence in Education. Viewing public education as anti-God and socialist in nature, Simonds strongly believes that "the battleground of testing for the church is in the public schools."

Virtually all Religious Right organizations profit from the work of Paul Weyrich, a communications expert. Through his National Empowerment Television organization, Weyrich keeps a steady flow of information going to Religious Right organizations nationwide. Credited with bringing both Jerry Falwell and Pat Robertson into the political arena, Weyrich once said, "This alliance between religion and politics didn't just happen; I've been working on it for years."[7]

The Mission of the Religious Right: Issues

Ralph Reed voiced the call that resounds among members of the Religious Right when he summoned Christians to be "followers of a humble carpenter from Galilee" and view politics as a "mission field."[8] On another occasion, Reed gave specific content to this general challenge, "What Christians have to do is to take back this country, one precinct at a time, one neighborhood at a time, and one state at a time."[9]

Increased involvement in politics coupled with occasions of obvious success for the Religious Right have expanded the range of issues to which members devote time and attention. No longer focused exclusively on religious issues, narrowly defined, the Religious Right speaks forcefully and acts influentially regarding a balanced federal budget, tax cuts, term limits for elected officials, and welfare reform. A study of the primary issues initiatives among major Religious Right organizations reveals at least five consensus issues held as high priorities by most everyone in the movement.

Abortion. Abortion remains the major social issue addressed by Religious Right organizations. James Dobson likens abortion practices in the United States to the Holocaust in Germany, "Hitler murdered 6,000,000 Jews; we in the United States have killed nearly 30,000,000 unborn babies."[10] Declaring that abortion is worse than the Holocaust, Pat Robertson told the 1995 Road to Victory conference of the Christian Coalition that people should do "whatever it takes" to get abortion outlawed.

With a kindred spirit, Randall Terry, founder of Operation Rescue in 1987, fights abortion in the halls of Congress, in the courts, at the front doors of abortion clinics, and in the streets. Terry admonished one congregation to which he spoke, "I want you to just let a wave of intolerance wash over you. I want you to let a wave of hatred wash over you. Yes, hate is good."[11] Little wonder that extremists in the anti-abortion movement even justify taking the lives of people who run abortion clinics in order to prevent additional abortions.

Public Education. Public education is a major "whipping boy" for Religious Right supporters. Convinced that "secular humanism" pervades public schools, Religious Right organizations work for reform in public education as they seek permission to channel public tax dollars into support for private education. Indicative of their commitment to the first goal, critics of public education support legislation that requires creationism be taught in science classes. As for public funding for private schools, campaigns to establish a voucher system of education persist.

Organizations such as Citizens for Excellence in Education condemn the generally respected National Education Association as an anti-Christian hate group. They oppose educational programs aimed at nurturing relaxation, creativity, and self-esteem, as well as all outcome-based methods of teaching. Arguing that New Age advocates manipulate public education to destroy children's faith in God and to lure them into seances and witchcraft, many of Robert Simonds' followers want to see public schools totally abolished. Jerry Falwell spoke out in support of this idea as early as 1979:

> I hope I live to see the day when, as in the early days of our country, we won't have any public schools. The churches will have taken them over again, and Christians will be running them.[12]

Prayer in Public Schools. Religious Right entities continue to devote massive amounts of time and attention to the issue of prayer in public schools. Spokespersons of the movement blame everything from the rise of a drug culture to increased criminal activities on Supreme Court decisions eliminating mandatory student participation in prepared prayers in public classrooms. Seldom, though, do advocates of mandatory prayer in public schools acknowledge that a student's freedom to offer a voluntary prayer in school never has been questioned, much less banned by anyone.

Family Values. Family values became a popular phrase during the 1992 presidential campaign. Devotees of the Religious Right continue to capitalize on the "virtuous" ring of this phrase as they give it their own special definitions. After all, who would not support family values?

But, what kind of family? And, which values? That's where the rub comes. Alongside traditional values such as honesty and fidelity, the Religious Right places issues such as defeating the United Nations Convention on the Rights of the Child, enacting a bill of parental rights, and supporting a requirement that prisoners make financial restitution to their victims before being released from confinement. Capping payments to welfare mothers stands right alongside enacting tougher laws against child pornography as a part of the movement's emphasis on family values.

The family values campaign attacks homosexuality with a vengeance. Beverly LaHaye cites the homosexual movement as the most serious threat to families and children of all the problems in America. In an even more vitriolic comment, Pat Robertson claims that "many of those people involved in Adolf Hitler were Satanists; many of them were homosexuals—the two things seem to go together." Religious Right activists call for a repeal of civil rights for gays and lesbians and the establishment of reparative therapy for all homosexuals.

Anti-Church-State Separation. Though leaders of the Religious Right ostensibly affirm the principle of religious liberty, they view the historic constitutional principle of church-state separation with great hostility. Robert Simonds dubbed the separationist tradition as "a socialist myth." Similarly, Pat Robertson argues that church-state separation is a "Soviet concept" not found in the teachings of the nation's founders, not historical, not a teaching of the law, and not a teaching of the Bible.

Keith Fournier, who runs Robertson's American Center for Law and Justice, likens Thomas Jefferson's metaphor of a wall of separation between church and state to Communist oppression as he persistently pleads, "Tear down the wall." Disdaining a guarantee of religious liberty for all citizens, Beverly LaHaye asserts,

Christian values should dominate our government. The test of those values is the Bible. Politicians who do not use the Bible to guide their public and private lives do not belong in office.[13]

The Method of the Religious Right: Strategies

Many of the older Religious Right organizations, such as Jerry Falwell's now defunct Moral Majority, worked for high visibility at the highest levels of national politics. Not satisfied with the minimal successes of their predecessors, new Religious Right organizations have developed state-of-the-art political strategies that reach into virtually every neighborhood in the nation. They complement traditional efforts in public education and political lobbying with a vast array of novel political strategies.

Cooperation. Religious Right organizations work together. Though the movement is far from monolithic, and disagreements between participants arise from time to time, Religious Right organizations cooperate with each other to give an appearance of amazing unanimity. Such cooperation produces a political bloc with sizable dimensions and powerful clout.

Grass-Roots Organization. Most of the earlier religiously conservative political organizations sought a national profile and serviced a national agenda. Today's Religious Right focuses on state and local politics. For example, Focus on the Family has formed political groups in thirty-five states.

Citizens for Excellence in Education works to establish an active Christian Parents Committee in every school district in the nation so as to gain a majority on the school board that can determine local policy, select curriculum, choose textbooks, and monitor programs and personnel.

The Christian Coalition resolved to take over the Republican Party by focusing its activities on precinct politics. Committed to placing a "precinct coordinator" and ten "helpers" in every one of the nation's 175,000 precincts, coalition members poured into poorly attended caucuses and other local meetings of the Republican Party and took over.

Use of Local Churches. Religious Right organizations use local churches to establish a foothold in various communities from which other work can be done. The Christian Coalition compares church rolls to lists of registered voters to identify people in a community whom they need to get registered to vote. Then, coalition strategists encourage churches to conduct "in-pew" voter registration drives just before or right after the offering is received during worship services. Religious Right groups have also found communication systems in local congregations to be invaluable means of getting people to the polls on election days.

Some Religious Right leaders recognize potential problems with these tactics. On the Sunday prior to a crucial election in San Diego in 1990, coalition members canvassed church parking lots across the city to place fliers on all the cars. However, leaders of this campaign instructed workers to wait until at least ten minutes after services had begun to begin their distribution lest latecomers to worship see what was happening and and end up "telling on you."

Distribution of Voter Guides. The Religious Right has found the use of legislative scorecards to be one of the most effective strategies for defeating incumbent candidates for state and national offices. Persons who prepare these scorecards identify several key pieces of legislation and explain how a positive or negative vote on each one signals a politician's sense of morals. If a vote in support of a particular bill represents admirable morality, a negative vote on that piece of legislation indicates the legislator should be removed from office. And, it works. Legislative scorecards have greatly impacted voters in recent presidential and congressional elections.

A recent mailing from the Christian Coalition profiles senators' and representatives' votes on family issues contained in congressional Republicans' 1995 "Contract with America." A set of symbols enables readers of the scorecard to identify whether or not a legislator voted "in favor" or "against" the "Christian Coalition's position."

As criteria for evaluating legislators' morals, the scorecard reports congressional votes on issues such as a balanced budget amendment, term limits, tax relief, anti-crime legislation, federal grants to abortion clinics, health care reform, lifting ban on gays in the military, promoting homosexuality to school children, voluntary school prayer, pornography on the internet, ban on immigrants with the HIV/AIDS virus, and prohibiting National Endowment of the Arts' grants to support artists who produce pornography.

Media. The titular head of the Religious Right is also an electronic-media mogul. Pat Robertson skillfully uses television to publicize and advance the causes of right-wing politics. Similarly, James Dobson promotes his organization and political views via a national radio ministry.

Less well-funded Religious Right organizations that cannot tap into electronic-media networks focus their efforts on the print media. Virtually every Religious Right organization regularly publishes a newsletter that reinforces emphases elaborated through carefully targeted direct mail campaigns. As a part of their pre-election work, organizational leaders publicize their candidates and issues by purchasing a full-page advertisement in the most influential newspaper among voters in an area.

Most leaders in the Religious Right have published major monographs that provide readers insight into their lives, interests, and political agendas.

Stealth Candidates. The Religious Right's encouragement of "stealth candidates" in local elections has proven to be one of the movement's most controversial political strategies. Leaders in the movement have instructed their candidates for local school boards, city councils, and positions in local political organizations to run for office without identifying their conservative religious ideas and affiliations.

In its 1992 "County Action Plan," the Pennsylvania Christian Coalition printed an italicized warning to its liaisons with the Republican Party who were seeking to become directly involved in local Republican committees: "You should never mention the name Christian Coalition in Republican circles."[14]

After the Christian Coalition came under intense criticism for its "stealth candidate" strategy, Pat Robertson repudiated the Pennsylvania document. However, Ralph Reed, Robertson's chosen leader for the Christian Coalition, had gone on record personally affirming a clandestine approach to political action. Although later Reed also repudiated his remark, the Coalition leader explained,

I want to be invisible. I do guerilla warfare. I paint my face and travel at night. You don't know it's over until you're in a body bag. You don't know until election night.[15]

Court Battles. Religious Right leaders argue their case in the courts as well as in churches and precincts. The American Center for Law and Justice aims to open an office in each of the nation's thirteen United States Court of Appeals judicial districts. Viewing itself as the Christian counterpart to the American Civil Liberties Union, this group takes high-profile court cases related to anti-abortion activities and religious exercises in public schools.

Personal Attacks. Frequently, supporters of the Religious Right's agenda allow ideological debates with opponents to deteriorate into personal attacks on these advocates of a different point of view. Political dissent is equated with a theological and spiritual error. Personal support for a bad idea, as defined by the Religious Right, qualifies one as a bad person.

Displeased with the administration of Bill Clinton, Jerry Falwell unleashed a vicious attack on the President. Utilizing the resources of his political lobbying organization, The Liberty Alliance, Falwell distributed a video entitled *Bill and Hilary Clinton's Circle of Power*—a product as dangerous as an assassin's bullet. Falwell marketed this video nationally by means of an infomercial that periodically replaced his "Old-Time Gospel Hour" on television. Aimed at discrediting the President, the video accuses Clinton of involvement in plane crashes, fires, break-ins, and murders among people collecting information against him.

And More. Numerous other strategies appear from time to time under the sponsorship of Religious Right organizations. The American Family Association often initiates consumer boycotts targeted at sponsors of objectionable television programming. Focus on the Family regularly sponsors church-based political training sessions known as "Community Impact Seminars." Repeatedly the Religious Right proves its expertise in amassing a database to support extensive direct mail campaigns.

Causes for Concern: A Brief Critique of the Religious Right

Many generalizations affirmed by the Religious Right comprise beneficial emphases within the Christian community: the need for
Christians to be involved in the political process, the importance of
biblical truths in national life, the significance of traditional family
values, the contributions that prayer can make to individuals' lives.
Serious concerns arise, however, in relation to several of the specific
programs and themes of the Religious Right as well as with the strategies employed to advance these emphases.

Attacks on Church-State Separation. As a church-based movement,
the Religious Right seeks more freedom to use the government for its
religious purposes and to use religion for its political purposes. Not
surprisingly, then, the movement views the United States Constitution's provision related to religious liberty with hostility and
vigorously works to alter it. Leading voices of the Religious Right
describe Thomas Jefferson's metaphor of a wall of separation between
church and state as "a socialist myth," "a lie to the left," "religious
cleansing," and "not a wall but a coffin."[16]

Ironically, the Religious Right enjoys the freedom to attack
church-state separation because of the very constitutional guarantee
that it would like to destroy. The Constitution's prohibition of an established religion and protection of freedom for religious expression
serve everyone well. Were the Religious Right to be successful in its
assault on the separationist wall, the big loser would be religion—the
church and all other religious organizations. In such a situation, the
ruling majority within the government at any given time would determine the appropriateness of religious practices.

Opposition to Public Education. Public education runs like a spinal
cord through the body politic. An effective democracy depends upon
an informed citizenry. The development of an informed citizenry
requires a public system of education available to everyone. Abol-
ishing public education would jeopardize the future health of the
nation in much the same manner that damaging the spinal cord para-
lyzes, if not kills, an individual.

Revisionist History. Much of the ballyhoo about recovering the United States' identity as a "Christian" nation rests on revisionist history. Founders of our nation adopted a secular constitution to establish a secular government. Fearful of limiting freedom, mentors of the nation even refused to endorse a statement of civil rights at first. The only reference to religion in the body of the Constitution forbids the application of a religious test in the determination of a candidate's qualifications for public office. When objections arose because of an absence of the name of God in the Constitution, James Madison explained that the document was intended to avoid even "a shadow of right in the general government to intermeddle with religion."[17]

Passionate pleas aside, a return to the much lamented "good old days" would not actually be very good from a religious point of view. Religion impacts the lives of today's citizens to a far greater extent than was the case in the early days of the nation when the state supported religion. Respected church historian Charles Handy documents a pervasive indifference to religion among patriots alive at the dawn of the nineteenth century. Constitutionally supported church-state separation protects the integrity of both the government and religion, thus potentially enhancing, rather than diminishing, the public's appreciation for both.

Some constituents of the Religious Right argue that Jefferson and Madison intended something very different from the present constitutional provision, but their assertions find no basis in facts. Jefferson repeatedly asserted that the sources of the law of the land were to be found in a body of law adopted and obeyed by people long before Jesus Christ appeared in history. Thus, these laws did not rest on Christian foundations. Jefferson stood by the statement he wrote into a letter in 1802:

> I contemplate with solemn reverence that act of the whole American people which declared that their legislature should "make no law respecting an establishment of religion, or prohibiting the free exercise thereof," thus building a wall of separation between Church and State.[18]

Madison, likewise, wrote to a Lutheran minister that a distinction between what is due to Caesar and what is due to God, best promotes the discharge of both obligations . . . A mutual independence is found most friendly to practical religion, to social harmony, and to political prosperity.[19]

A Short-Sighted View of Freedom. From the vantage point of a member of a majority supportive of a prevailing point of view, arguing to legislate the will of the majority looks good. Seen from a minority position threatened by the majority, however, the whole matter looks differently. Real security requires rights for the minority that equal rights claimed by the majority.

Currently, in the name of freedom, the Religious Right supports policies that threaten the freedom of citizens who hold differing views. Leaders in the movement fail to see that only when freedom is available to everyone can they continue to enjoy freedom even when, if ever, they become a minority.

Would members of the Christian Coalition living in a Buddhist-dominated school district favor the imposition of a Buddhist prayer on their children attending public schools? Would a supporter of the American Family Association applaud the censorship of Christian values in public media because of an anti-Christian government? Would a member of Focus on the Family be comfortable with a definition of family that completely overlooks the traditional family unit? Would constituents of the Christian Coalition accept exclusion from the political process based on their affiliation with the Republican Party?

Unless all persons are free, no one is really free. As long as freedom depends upon a particular majority, freedom knows no stability.

Morally Suspect Strategies. Another name for stealth candidates is political dishonesty that, like dishonesty of any kind, is wrong. Candidates for elected offices have a moral responsibility to be truthful about whom they represent and for what they stand. To cover up such data until after an election debunks political integrity.

Attempts at character assassination also raise serious moral questions. Ideas can be debated apart from efforts to destroy individuals on the other side of the debate.

The Religious Right's close alignment with the Republican Party qualifies as a highly questionable strategy. Can people support the

Religious Right's agenda only from within that one political party? Should all people who vote as Democrats or Independents be considered irreligious? Identifying a Christian agenda with the sectarian politics of one particular body is dangerous at best.

The Rhetoric of War. During his 1992 bid to gain the Republican Party's nomination for the presidency of the United States, Patrick Buchanan announced the existence of a "cultural war for the soul of our country." Later, during the Christian Coalition's 1993 annual conference, Buchanan returned to this theme declaring,

> I am not here to talk surrender terms, but to talk about how to fight and win the cultural war. Our culture is superior . . . because our religion is Christianity.[20]

Similarly, Paul Weyrich had told the 1992 assembly of Christian Coalition members, "We are in a war."[21] Subsequently Weyrich created the C-NET (Coalition's National Empowerment Television), explaining that in any war the generals first address the issue of communication.

Others in the Religious Right movement use a similarly militant rhetoric. Frankly, much of it does not sound very Christian. In 1991, Pat Robertson described his work in a membership drive as "raising an army."[22] Earlier Robertson had employed a different metaphor with an equally violent portent to announce the arrival of a time "for a godly fumigation" to get rid of "the termites" destroying institutions that have been built by Christians.[23]

Ralph Reed, of the Christian Coalition, described his organization's work as a form of "guerilla warfare" that ends up with opponents "in a body bag" before they know what has happened to them.[24] Such imagery is consistent with that of Billy Falling, who in his book *The Political Mission of the Church*, a volume recommended and marketed by Citizens for Excellence in Education, commissioned the government to serve as "the police department" within God's kingdom on earth. According to Falling, the government should be ready at any moment to "impose God's vengeance upon those who abandon God's laws of justice."[25]

In a volatile, violent culture, even metaphorical references to combat can cause major problems. Only a childishly short step separates the rhetoric of war from war-like actions. Grisly proof of that reality existed outside an abortion clinic in Pensacola, Florida, where a zealot for "God's truth" exacted "moral" vengeance on persons who disagreed with his convictions, leaving two of them dead.

Beyond Criticism: A Call to Action

Much about the Religious Right merits criticism, but not everything. Overreacting to religious organizations seeking political influence jeopardizes the wisdom of learning from religious values. Caution is an appropriate response, but to disregard good ideas simply because they come from religion-oriented sources represents a serious mistake.

In the late 1960s and early 1970s, liberal Democrats displayed no discomfort with religious language. Opponents of the war in Vietnam and proponents of civil rights legislation conveyed their political convictions in the terminology of Christian morality. Indeed, the civil rights movement was a church-based movement that utilized the vocabulary, litanies, and hymns of Christian congregations.

Once conservative Christian groups launched their political initiatives in the 1980s, however, religious language became the prerogative of Republicans. Democrats disdained political ideas articulated by means of religious rhetoric. Talk about throwing out the baby with the bath water!

Paranoia about religion on the part of the government is as unhealthy in a democracy as a religion's passion to control the government. Good ideas are good ideas regardless of their source or the language in which they are communicated. Our government need no more be hostile to religion than submissive to religion. A dialogue between religion and government can benefit all of us.

The popularity of the Religious Right indicates the public's pervasive hunger for morals to exercise a significant influence in the political arena. The great issues of our time have a moral dimension that can benefit from religious perspectives.

Religion has a valid word to offer to politicians. In reality, the whole society will be worse off should religious influences not be a part of the mix out of which major political decisions are made.

Religion has a rightful, helpful place in the public square; it just can't be an altar before which the government makes all people bow. It is not enough to criticize the Religious Right. Anyone can throw stones. An honest critique of the agenda of the Religious Right should be complemented by suggestions on alternative methods by which morals can play an important role in political discussions.

Government needs input from the Christian community. Politics benefit from an engagement with Christian morals. As Stephen Carter observed,

> If the Christian Coalition is wrong for America, it must be because its message is wrong on the issues, not because its message is religious.[26]

The real danger of the Christian Coalition resides not in its religiosity but in its political platform and methodology.

How can we move beyond the present confusion surrounding faith and politics to insure integrity in Christians' political activities?

Jesus laid down a principle of Christian citizenship that, if heeded, prevents any confusion regarding the relationship between faith and politics. In an imperative without ambiguity, Jesus told his disciples to give the government what belongs to the government and to give to God what belongs to God. Implicit in this statement about the realm of faith and the world of politics was a stern warning: never confuse the two.

Faithful obedience to the mandate from Jesus delivers us from investing in the government a level of interest, passion, trust, and devotion that belongs only to God; from seeking to use the government to do the work of faith; and from transforming the body of Christ into a partisan political power bloc.

Two Crucial Questions

Early in this section of the book, I pointed to a question that, if answered correctly, can lead us out of the present confusion—How *is*

God honored in the political process? Asked in a more personal manner, the inquiry is: How is God honored by Christian citizens?

God is honored by political organizations and actions that work diligently to assure freedom for all people, to house the homeless, to guarantee justice, to feed the hungry, to strike down prejudice, to pursue peace, and to provide the benefits of society to everyone in it. Logically, then, God is honored by Christian citizens who work at every level of the political process as advocates for and architects of a government with such sensitivity and integrity.

No special provisions exist for Christians involved in politics, and none should be expected. Democracy works most efficiently when the same rules apply to all citizens. If a group of Christians forms a political action coalition, members of that organization must abide by the same regulations on financial disclosure, lobbying ethics, and other activities that apply to all political action groups. A Christian individual who runs for public office must be willing to serve all the public, not just those persons who agree with a particular religious confession.

Functioning in the realm of politics as "servants of God" is no justification for breaking laws without accepting the consequences of criminal behavior, expecting privileges without paying dues, or violating governmental procedures apart from reprimands. Christians who work as political activists have to abide by majority votes the same as do all other politicians. Though majority votes cannot determine morality, they do set policies that, until changed, command compliance by Christian citizens.

The political morality that honors God centers on fidelity not winning, faithfulness rather than victories. Christians enter the realm of politics with a measure of freedom not enjoyed by all persons who work in civil affairs. Faith allows defeat and wipes away the fear of losing. As a matter of faith, Christian citizens support durable principles that are worthy of support even at the expense of losing a vote. God is honored by, and honors, fidelity.

The Way Out Is the Way In

The very words from Jesus quoted by many people to justify political involvements that have deepened the confusion between faith and politics are the same words that, if properly heeded, can clear up that confusion. Obedience to the imperative from Jesus slices through a messed-up situation like nothing else and identifies appropriate behavior for Christians within the civil arena.

Christians—persons who give to God what is God's—have a role to play in government. Faith has political responsibilities (to give to the state what the state is due). Rightly understood, faith and politics interact with each other. Worship God and serve the government; but don't ever confuse faith and politics or allow either to become dependent upon the other. Obedience to the words of Jesus brings clarity to the proper relationship between politics and faith like nothing else.

Notes

[1] David Cantor, *The Religious Right: The Assault on Tolerance & Pluralism in America* (New York: Anti-Defamation League, 1994) 61.

[2] Ibid., 15.

[3] Ibid., 63.

[4] Ibid., 27.

[5] *Christianity Today*, 17 July 1995, 54.

[6] *U.S. News & World Report*, 24 April 1995, 34.

[7] Cantor, 93.

[8] Warren Fiske, "GOP Hopefuls Praise Potential Kingmaker," *The Virginian-Pilot*, 9 September 1995, A9

[9] Cantor, 27.

[10] Ibid., 81.

[11] Ibid., 118.

[12] Ibid., 6.

[13] Ibid., 107.

[14] Ibid., 32.

[15] Ibid., 31.

[16] Robert Boston and Joseph L. Conn, "The Extremist World View Behind Pat Robertson's Media Empire," *Extra*, March/April 1995, 14.

[17] Robert Boston, *Why the Religious Right is Wrong about Separation of Church & State* (New York: Prometheus Books, 1993) 62.

[18] Thomas Jefferson, letter to the Danbury Baptist Association, 1 January 1802, included in Charles C. Haynes, *Religion in American History: What to Teach and How* (Alexandria VA: Association for Supervision and Curriculum Development, 1990) 48.

[19] Ralph Ketcham, *James Madison: A Biography* (Charlottesville VA: University Press of Virginia, 1971) 167.

[20]Cantor, 40.
[21]Ibid., 33.
[22]Ibid., 30.
[23]Ibid., 26.
[24]Ibid., 31.
[25]Ibid., 104.
[26]Stephen L. Carter, *The Culture of Disbelief: How American Law and Politics Trivialize Religious Devotion* (New York: Doubleday, 1994) 266.

Part II

FAITH
and
POLITICS

Questioning the
Relationship Between
Christian Convictions
and Political Platforms

Notes from a Personal Pilgrimage

"We just vote for the man," they said. "His political party doesn't matter. We're not Democrats or Republicans, just Christians trying to elect a good man to office." So went the election-time litany regularly repeated by most members in the church of my childhood. Their rhetoric squared with reality. Often preceding a fall election, political supporters of a Republican candidate for the national presidency favored a Democrat seeking to serve the state as governor. The next time around, their votes went to an Independent.

"We just vote for the man." In earlier days, that declaration impressed me as independent-minded and morally responsible. Eventually, though, I realized that, like it or not, the candidate's party comes with the candidate (especially in elections at the national and state levels of government).

Every politician has a political platform—announced or hidden, organized or developed on the spot. Regardless of how "nice" a candidate seems, how empathetic with the common people she appears, or how religious he sounds, unless that candidate's political platform represents what's best for the office sought and reflects voters' values, the person does not merit election. Reaching responsible decisions about a politician's platform, however, necessitates voters' developing a political platform of their own.

My first thoughts about a personal political platform brought me face to face with inconsistencies and confusion in my religious tradition. A few issues mattered more than others, but I was not sure they were the right issues to be used as criteria for evaluating a candidate. I really didn't know the outline, priorities, or basic principles of my political beliefs, but I knew I had to find out.

Cleaning up Bad Morals

The religious tradition that informed and nurtured my early years placed a premium on political issues that impacted private morals. Congregations that hid behind a misunderstanding of church-state separation in an effort to avoid addressing major social problems readily (and sometimes carelessly) ventured into political movements aimed at regulating various facets of personal moral behavior. The most popular planks in the political platform, though never defined as such, among my Christian friends consisted of support for Sunday closing laws and opposition to the sale of alcoholic beverages.

Even the good folks in my past who stayed away from politics as a matter of conscience quickly set aside their reservations about political involvement when faced by the challenge of a local option election. An official call for a county-wide vote on the legal status of liquor sales, Sunday closing policies, or gambling congealed Christians into a formative political force. Given the right issue, my "non-political" Christian friends did efficient political organization and impassioned political campaigning as well as anyone. Even local church pulpits, usually considered off-limits for political declarations, hosted fiery denunciations of opponents and loudly trumpeted support for the politics of righteousness.

Confessing Inconsistency

During one of my early pastorates, I watched the same Christians who campaigned vigorously against a liquor-by-the-drink referendum in our community refuse even to address a proposed piece of open-housing legislation. Christian citizens irate about a zoning change that allowed construction of a tavern in their neighborhood demonstrated no concern at all for a referendum related to funding a facility for troubled young people.

Such inconsistency implied an imbalanced concept of morality—personal morality is more important than social morality. Christians had no problem entering a political fray to address personal moral concerns, but pressing moral problems in society seemed out of bounds.

One day, after I had spoken to a group of state legislators in Alabama, an elected representative voiced his frustration with the political inconsistency of the religious community:

> If we are about to vote on a gambling issue, I can't walk down the halls of the Capitol building because of the press of Christian people lobbying us to refute gambling. And, that's alright. I'm glad to have their support for such a vote. But I have been working for years to pass penal reform legislation that would correct an inhumane treatment of criminals, and I can't get a single one of these Christians to lift a voice on behalf of my efforts. The same can be said about dozens of other pieces of critically needed social legislation.

Broadening the Agenda

A balanced political platform for a Christian includes both private and social concerns. Sensitized by biblical morality, Christians do not have the luxury of focusing only on political issues of personal interest. University and seminary professors such as Henlee H. Barnett, one of the persons to whom this book is dedicated, challenged whatever remnants of a narrow moral agenda that remained in me. Through a careful study of the Scriptures, I became interested in an ever-widening expanse of issues of importance in the political arena. Concerns related to personal morality remained, but new interests emerged—for example, civil rights, racial equality, economic justice, crime, penal reform, foreign policy, environmental regulations, and government ethics.

Presently I find it necessary to look at candidates for public office from a variety of different perspectives. Each point of view develops out of a dialogue between my own moral convictions, political values, and social conscience. From my political platform, I study the political platforms of others.

Can morality be legislated?

Obviously morality differs from public policy. Laws emerge from legislative assemblies made up of fallible people. Christian morality develops out of the pages of the Bible that contain the wisdom of Almighty God. Secular institutions enforce civil law, threatening state-inflicted penalties for those who disobey it. The people of God propagate Christian morality, commending moral integrity as a way to abundant life and warning that moral irresponsibility results in spiritual brokenness. Civil courts pass judgments on laws. God alone is capable of judging an individual's moral disposition. Obviously, morality differs from public policy, even though morality and civil law are integrally related.

Historically, most laws represent the codification of someone's morality. The Western world found that deriving specific civil laws from general moral principles—such as truth, justice, and freedom—protected the state from the whims of every political leader who came along wanting to legislate his own particular values. Christians have seen basic tenets of Christian morality embraced in legislative actions. Indeed, the great reformer Martin Luther referred to civil law as one of the "masks of God."

Which Morality?

No question exists about the possibility of legislating morality. It can be done; and it is done all the time. A more fundamental question asks *which* morality to legislate? That inquiry prods yet another question: What morality is it *possible* to legislate?

Basic moral principles that contribute to a better quality of life for all citizens provide legitimate content for civil laws. Individual or sectarian moral beliefs may not offer promise for everyone, though. Thankfully, fundamental moral insights regarding the dignity and worth of every individual have given rise to civil laws prohibiting acts such as murder and domestic abuse. However, an individual's moral convictions regarding the relationship between personal dignity and personal grooming do not serve as a proper foundation for far-reaching public policies. Ethical convictions on the sanctity of worship and the importance of religious instruction have precipitated federal laws protecting the freedom of both. But one religious group's moral concept of the manner in which worship should take place and the content of indoctrination must not be imposed on others.

Laws exist to serve justice, not a particular point of view. Thus, the morality that best informs public policy derives from fundamental ethical precepts that contribute to the common good without violating personal or religious freedom.

Caution! Abuses

Some people are always hard at work to make their particular moral convictions normative for the nation by means of federal legislation. At the same time, other individuals seek to use the basic principles of Christian morality as devices to further their own political philosophy. Each of these efforts represents an abuse of both morality and the law.

Sectarian groups have a perfect right to exercise their moral convictions and to propagate them publicly, but such groups do not have the right to impose their moral tradition's bill of particulars on the rest of society. Franklin Littell aptly argued that a religion unable to win its case and grow on its own merits is not worthy of a future.1 Democracy welcomes the counsel of sectarian morality. A domination by sectarian morality helps nobody, however.

The second abuse develops as persons wed concepts of Christian morality to tenets of a partisan political philosophy. Often the ideals, language, and methods of this effort appear harmless (maybe even beneficial) on the surface. In reality, though, Christian morality gets prostituted in pursuit of a political goal. Christians must guard against persons and organizations using Christians' interests and activities to further their own political aspirations.

Don't Expect Too Much or Too Little

A given law may or may not embrace Christian morality. That is why Christians must respect the law while neither expecting too much from it or taking it too lightly. No court, judge, legislature, council, or elected official can ultimately determine what is moral and what is not. Honoring the law is not to be confused with unquestioning obedience to the law—the former is commended by the Bible; the latter is prohibited as a form of idolatry.

Laws can regulate behavior and contribute to the character of a nation, but laws cannot enforce right motives—a central concern in Christian morality. Christian morality can influence legislation and be promulgated through laws, but the future of Christian morality does not depend upon enactments of public policy.

What are some specific sources from which I can get help in formulating my political convictions?

Information garnered from a balanced sampling of print and electronic media, coupled with common sense, provides helpful insights for making decisions on political issues that have nothing to do with morality. However, when trying to reach conclusions about matters with strong moral underpinnings, overtones, and ramifications, several different types of resource materials should be consulted. Here are five good sources of insight with which to begin:

The Bible

Personally, accepting the Bible as the authoritative word of God, I consult the Bible as I construct or revise various planks in my political platform. Though the Bible is in no sense a moral code book, the Scriptures elaborate basic moral principles that apply to many contemporary issues.

Indirect Influence. The Bible is a book of faith—a God-inspired book written by people of faith for people of faith and people in search of faith. It is not a textbook on morals, politics, and society. The Bible alerts its readers to basic moral values—love, justice, mercy, forgiveness, honesty, and rest; to name a few. However, the Bible offers no specific direction for the application of these values to complex situations such as the wisdom of providing the President a line-item veto in the federal budget, whether or not American troops should be deployed to Bosnia, and a choice of the best method to secure Medicare benefits for generations to come. Turning to the Bible for help in formulating political strategies is akin to consulting a political action manual for insights into the nature of the Christian faith.

The Bible shapes people of conscience, individuals sensitive to moral values in their decision-making and character development. Since character, in turn, shapes conduct, the Bible's nurture of character represents the greatest moral benefit of the Bible.

Direct Influence. The Bible directly addresses specific issues that repeatedly appear in the political realm. Specific biblical texts convey authoritative judgments on issues such as marriage, capital punishment, war, and help for the poor. Each biblical text reflects its particular setting within the history of salvation, however. Thus, the counsel of an Old Testament passage may differ substantially from a teaching from Jesus. Biblical ethics and Christian ethics are not synonymous.

Under the banner of "family values," enthusiastic reconstructionists influenced by R. J. Rushdoony want to establish the death penalty for crimes (sins) such as adultery. From a biblical perspective, such a policy seems in order when viewed from Leviticus but reprehensible when placed under the light of Jesus' message. On the whole matter of sexual relations, the Bible contains not one but several different points of view (compare Gen 2, Song of Songs, Prov 7, Lev 19, 1 Cor 7, and 1 Pet 3).

One Voice among Many. Seldom does the Bible present one well-defined moral norm that has received precisely the same treatment in all periods of the history of faith. More often than not, the Bible offers several perspectives on an issue and prompts fundamental questions that should be raised when studying that issue.

Turning to the Bible for insight in the development of political positions is important, but further study is necessary. We also need to know how an issue in question has fared throughout church history.

Church History

The church is the only "community that undertakes to relate Christians' specific moral choices and acts to their identity *as Christians*."[2] Thus a knowledge of how the church has treated an issue across the ages can helpfully inform contemporary Christians dealing with that issue in the process of formulating a political platform.

The Church and Morality. The church preserves and conveys moral traditions. Much of church history consists of the church's interpretation and application of the Bible in thoughts, words, and actions (evangelical missions, liturgical forms, and political initiatives). Contemporary considerations of moral issues benefit greatly from studying the fate of these issues within Christian communities across the centuries.

Consistent Inconsistency. Any review of church history consistently documents the inconsistency with which the church has treated major issues. Take war, for example.

Based upon the teachings of the New Testament and the example of Jesus, early Christians apparently embraced pacifism with a passion. Prior to 170–180 A.D., no evidence exists that Christians served in armed forces.[3] During the first three centuries of the Christian church, all outstanding Christian writers in both the East and West repudiated participation in warfare on the part of Christians.[4] By no means, however, have Christians maintained this anti-war posture through the centuries.

A review of official resolutions and pronouncements in my own denomination reveal an insistence on peace prior to a declaration of war on the part of Congress or the President. After an official declaration, though, denominational leaders have urged church members to support the military efforts of their government. Frequently, national patriotism has appeared more important than allegiance to a moral value commended and practiced by Jesus.

On most political issues, a singular biblical position or a distinctly defined Christian position is nonexistent. Yet, both the Bible and the church enable Christian decision-makers (and political platform builders) to view various ideological options with discretion and a sensitivity to moral values. Constructing a responsible political platform, though, requires studies that move beyond religious materials.

Political Statements

Politicians spell out their convictions on various issues in statements for the media, in posturing speeches, in printed reports to voters, and in position papers distributed by their offices. A comparison of differing political perspectives on the same issue can help us form a personal opinion about that issue.

Additional help can be found by contacting the national headquarters of various special interest groups. The organization, Citizens for Excellence in Education, provides a wealth of material critical of public schools. A radically different point of view on the same topic can be secured from the National Education Association.

Both the Democratic Party and the Republican Party offer interpretive materials on their priorities. Studying materials from each major political party side-by-side can clarify differences in their philosophies and strategies and enable us to reach better informed conclusions of our own.

Expert Opinions

Expert opinions prove extremely beneficial in political decision-making, especially when an expert speaks or writes in the field of his or her expertise. Otherwise, watch out.

Truth or Propaganda. Propagandists regularly secure a popular expert in one field to speak authoritatively regarding an issue in a completely different field. The hope is that a gullible public, which generally respects the speaker's authority, will fail to note that, on this occasion, her comments address a matter outside her realm of authority. A woman's status as an attractive, skilled actress endows her with no special competence to advocate a particular position on a controversial piece of environmental legislation. Sometimes a comment billed as an honest expert's opinion is no more than a slick attempt at propaganda.

Reaching a personal conclusion about economic policies requires a study of different economic philosophies. Expert economists provide helpful information. Likewise, developing an opinion on welfare necessitates consideration of the suggestions of social scientists and actual caseworkers. The insights of military strategists prove invaluable in the development of a defense budget, but negotiators and diplomats are the best advisors on initiatives for peace.

Dealing with Bias. No one is unbiased, experts included. A careful massage of raw data can make identical facts look very different. Numerical statistics lend themselves to a vast array of interpretations and manipulations. Thus, on any issue, we should consult more than one expert opinion. We make our best decision on a matter once we have achieved a balanced perspective on it.

Personal Observations

Don't underestimate the power of common sense and personal observations as sources of political insight. The real test of a policy statement, a campaign promise, or the legislative initiatives of an individual candidate is effect—effect on people. In the final analysis, good intentions don't count. Historically, many well-motivated acts ended up hurting people horrendously.

Seeing a policy's impact on specific persons tells the true story of that policy's worth. Cutbacks in welfare expenditures seem wise and right until we realize that these reductions take away a hot-meals program targeted at hungry kids. Calls for Medicare reform sound appealing until a citizen watches one of her parents denied needed medication because of a change in Medicare policies. State-sponsored gambling carries the appearance of a quick fix for improving local economic resources until the public witnesses the dramatic rise in bankruptcies, embezzlements, and family problems that accompany a proliferation of gambling establishments in an area.

In formulating a set of political beliefs, we do well not only to study policies on various issues but to look carefully at how these policies impact specific individuals. Personal observations provide priority information.

What moral principles best inform the development of a Christian's political platform?

No aspect of developing a political platform is more difficult or more crucial than bringing values to bear on goals. Indeed, many thoughtful people contend that "reconnecting politics to our best values is now the most important task of political life."[5]

A few moral principles receive near consensus endorsement among Christians. Even when individual believers radically disagree over how these principles should be applied to society, they still agree on the primacy of the principles themselves. These principles best instruct political decisions and shape political actions.

A word of caution is important. Christians rightly insist that Christian moral principles inform the development of a believer's political platform. It is terribly dangerous, however, to equate any one set of convictions influenced by these principles as "the" Christian political platform. Christians exhibit as much disagreement over the political application of moral principles as they do consensus on the necessity of heeding the wisdom of these principles.

Love and Justice

That Christianity begins with love, points toward love, calls for love, and thrives on love hardly anyone disputes. The salvation in which Christians rejoice springs from God's love for all people. The highest form of social interaction consists of loving relationships. Paul was writing moral theory as well as theology when he declared love as the greatest of all gifts.

Politics, however, present a serious challenge to love. Institutions, like government, can act in ways considered loving, but institutions cannot love. Love is a personal phenomenon—what people do that inanimate entities have no capacity for doing. So, in its social and political expression, love works with institutions to guarantee justice. Classically defined, justice requires that each person receive his or her due. Love moves justice beyond individuality to establish norms within society, however. There, justice works for the common good of all people, insisting on equality and advocating liberty and rights.

Selfishness is to love what self-interest is to the common welfare—a problem. Yet, self-interests form the fuel that keeps political machinery running. Contentions between different self-interests comprise the dynamics of political life. Government has a responsibility to order competing self-interests in a manner that causes them to support what justice demands. Christians, in turn, have a responsibility to nurture that kind of government.

A commitment to justice assures decisions and actions of a loving nature in a society and through a government made up of many people who may not be very loving. Love supports laws and institutions that establish and enforce justice. Even in situations where justice provides less than love would give, justice serves as a tool of love.

Freedom and Responsibility

Freedom is a big issue for Christians. Christians worship the God repeatedly revealed in movements of liberation. They recognize as Lord the Christ who rejected all forms of enslavement and coercion. Authentic faith develops only when an individual can exercise her free will. Real faith cannot be required, imposed, or enforced. Christian growth requires personal freedom in decision-making, character formation, and social action.

Freedom is also a big issue for governments, arguably, the fundamental goal of good government. Thus, politics, or the art of government, achieves its highest end when dedicated to the establishment and preservation of freedom—freedom for all citizens. Well-intentioned politicians pursue a government interested in the provision of individual rights and civil liberties, with no exceptions.

But, toward what end? The goal of freedom is not libertinism (a disregard for all law) or irresponsibility. Freedom provides citizens an opportunity to reach their fullest potential personally and to contribute positively to society. In other words, true freedom embraces responsibility. Liberated citizens are not free from responsibility, but free for responsibility. Indeed, responsibility contributes to the perpetuation of freedom even as freedom makes possible responsible action.

Personalism and Institutionalism

People come first. Individuals, not institutions, are created in the image of God, who endows every person with inestimable value. Thus, as William Temple pointed out long ago, "The primary principle of Christian ethics and Christian politics must be respect for every person as a person."[6]

Government exists for people, not vice versa. Institutions that do not serve citizens have no reason to exist. Likewise, the key criterion in evaluating governmental policies and procedures, legislative action, and social programs takes the form of a question: What does it do to people? We make better political decisions when we can see the faces and sense the needs of the people who will be most affected by the decisions made.

The principle of personalism may seem to conflict with the idea of the common good, at least occasionally. No "collective good" can be really "good," however, if it violates the dignity and welfare of individual persons.

Stewardship and Ownership

Though the word "steward" seldom appears in the Bible, the concept of stewardship stands at the center of God-pleasing life as described by biblical writers. At a minimum, good stewardship involves a recognition that all of life is a gift from God. From that realization comes the conclusion that no one really "owns" anything; everything is a trust to be used responsibly. The quality of our stewardship reflects the morality of our attitudes and actions.

Ownership is a prerogative of God. Trusteeship is the lot of individuals created in the image of God, which means everyone. Good stewards function as co-workers with God. Individuals view their possessions as means of service and value the earth as a gift to be preserved. Responsible trusteeship involves protecting and developing all that God entrusts to us in a manner consistent with God's purpose as revealed in creation and in Christ.

Means and Ends

In some systems of ethics, good ends justify whatever means people find necessary to accomplish them, but not in Christian ethics. From the perspective of biblical morality, the means and ends of moral actions reciprocally interact; each affects the other constructively or destructively. Employing immoral methods to accomplish a moral purpose strips that purpose of its value.

An "ends-justify-the-means" approach to political action is wrong whether the advocate is an old communist theoretician or a theologian recently aligned with the Religious Right. In the tradition of Trotsky, who argued that a good end justifies any means, Lenin established the continuation of communism as the basis for moral decision-making. Subsequently hard-line communists determine the moral nature of lies, slander, intimidation, and violence on the basis of whether or not they advance the communist cause. How different is that mentality from the perspective that abortions must be halted by whatever means necessary? Both are wrong.

Attaining a lofty social goal by means of unethical behavior taints the whole endeavor. Christians advocate morally sound goals achieved by morally responsible methods.

An Uneasy Obedience

Although most Christians agree on the importance of these fundamental moral principles, not all Christians hold identical political beliefs. Obviously, Christians develop vastly different political platforms.

Middle Axioms. Controversy arises at the point of bridging the gap between basic moral principles and the social problems and personal decisions to which these principles must be addressed. A virtually unanimous affirmation of moral values among Christians does not prevent dramatically diverse points of view once Christians apply the general values to specific situations.

Recognizing the leap involved in moving from the affirmation of a moral value to the application of that value to a specific political question, John Bennett developed the concept of "middle axioms." Bennett started with basic moral precepts, and then he questioned what each moral principle dictated in response to specific social situations. In each instance, Bennett arrived at a middle axiom—"more concrete than a universal ethical principle and less specific than a program that includes legislation and political strategy."[7]

Call it what you will, every person makes such a transition from the general to the specific. Variety in political platforms appears as individual Christians address issues such as economics, ecology, and peace on the basis of values such as love, justice, and stewardship. Political convictions represent a variation on middle axioms.

Competing Values. Occasionally political situations draw several moral principles into competition with one another. That creates a real dilemma for moral decision-makers. A sincere desire to do "the right thing" results in serious confusion regarding which "right thing" carries the highest priority.

In a racist society, for example, businesses may regularly ignore the issues of credentials and competence to bypass members of a racial minority in employment and professional development practices. Justice requires a correction of this situation. But how?

Legislating quotas to incorporate more minorities into the workforce seems like a desirable goal, but such legislation often results in reverse discrimination (discrimination against the racial majority). Employment policies consider an individual's race more important than his or her educational and technical qualifications for a job. Should a somewhat unjust regulation be established in the interest of correcting past injustices and establishing racial justice? Interests in fairness, equality, and personalism get all mixed up.

Honest Humility. Anyone who has attempted to bridge the chasm between biblical mandates and social problems knows the difficulty of that stretch. If the architecture for spanning this ideological canyon were clear and its construction easy, all Christians would come out at the same place. But we don't, obviously. Faced by competing values, believers exhibit different priorities. Even the application of a single guiding principle gets complicated by a crowd of other factors—economic biases, professional interests, personal prejudices, family political loyalties. About the best anyone can do is try to reflect the integrity of moral convictions in political decisions. Having done that, though, honesty requires a recognition that any one of us could be as wrong in our application of morality to politics as we tend to think others are in theirs. Humility comes easily when examining political agendas and studying political actions. Such humility serves everyone well.

What are the most important issues for Christians to consider in developing a political position on economic justice?

Economics occupies a position of primal importance among United States citizens. Both individuals and institutions, families and corporations, feel the consequences of governmental decisions about interest rates, the size of the national debt, a balanced budget, and adjustments in tax laws. National economic policies directly impact the number of other issues that can be addressed by the government and the manner as well as the quality of treatment devoted to these issues.

Guiding Principles

Christians benefit from an abundance of literature on morality and economics. Both the Bible and church history provide helpful perspectives on economic priorities and responsibilities.

The Nature of Wealth. Money is amoral. Wealth has no status as a criterion for judging morality. Neither poverty nor affluence automatically equates with good or evil. The quantity of a person's (or a nation's) economic resources is not indicative of the quality of that individual's (or entity's) moral integrity.

Attitudes toward wealth and the actions these attitudes inspire are another matter. Here moral interests abound. To establish wealth as the chief criterion in personal or social decision-making jeopardizes moral integrity, or compromises it completely. Profit takes precedence over service. A preoccupation with possible gains obstructs a vision of goods that should be shared. Materialism becomes an addiction.

Though, theoretically, most Christians reject the Marxist theory of economic determinism, in daily practices, many Christians embrace the economic theory that Karl Marx elaborated in *Das Kapital*. Disdaining other political views, an individual votes for a candidate because "she will be best for my business." A political action group calls for serious cuts in welfare subsidies because "helping those people takes money out of our pockets and they could do better if they wanted to." A philosopher muses that the nation may need some form of foreign conflict because wars always help the economy. Economic determinism!

When individuals or institutions use their possessions to accomplish worthwhile goals, wealth functions as an invaluable tool of morality. Conversely, when people or governments posit an accumulation of possessions as an end itself, affluence becomes a symbol of immorality.

Competition and Compassion. Many scholars credit Protestant piety, especially the work-ethic found in Calvinism, for the rise of capitalism. Free competition forms the cornerstone of a capitalistic economy. Competition in the market place increases sales, produces sizable profits, and generally increases everyone's standard of living—so the argument goes.

Ethicists within the Christian church have tended to view capitalism negatively. Critics claim that this economic system encourages greed, non-democratic decisions, monopolistic power, irresponsible ecology, commercialism, and social inequalities.8 Obviously, such developments conflict with the kind of compassion for other people commended by Christ.

Good alternatives to capitalism do not come easily, however. Socialism, an economic system ideologically committed to equality, community, justice, and freedom—all of which sound attractive to Christians—fares poorly in historical reality. Marxist thought idealizes socialism as the economic means for building a just society, but the actual results of Marxist economics reflect more evil than good.

An application of compassion to economic concerns usually results either in support for capitalism modified by some form of a welfare state or an endorsement of democratic socialism. Students of society recognize that in a free market economy not everyone enjoys a profit. Some people, in fact, get completely squeezed out of the system and require assistance.

The big questions prompted by an effort to balance economic competition and Christian compassion revolve around the subject of government intervention in the economic system. True *laissez-faire* capitalism requires the government to maintain a "hands off" policy related to economic interests. Government officials allow the financial dynamics of competing self-interests to bring about good results. Historically, Christians have had problems with such a non-regulated approach to economics. Compassion for troubled neighbors prods support for a government aggressive in correcting economic abuses and guaranteeing all people rights to food, clothing, shelter, health care, and education.

The Bottom Line. In Christian thought, the purpose of economics is the humanization of life. *Things* exist to make life better for *persons*— all persons. Economic strategies that use people, enslave people, and dehumanize people are immoral. Moral evaluations of economic policies focus not on profits but people—how the economy serves the citizenry, not vice versa.

Political Questions

The federal government sets much of the economic agenda for citizens. One set of questions addresses the federal budget itself: Should we adopt a constitutional amendment mandating a balanced federal budget? Should the President possess the power to exercise a line-item veto in the federal budget? How should this budget be monitored?

Questions related to taxes involve every level of government: Is a sales tax a fair tax? Should food and drugs be taxed? Do I favor the current system of taxation, or would I consider a flat tax?

Interest in daily work raises questions: How would I protect retirement income? How much involvement should the government have in regulating the work place? How should we assist the unemployed and underemployed? Can we help victims of hostile corporate takeovers? Much work in our country depends upon charitable giving, prompting such questions as these: Would I protect a tax deduction for charitable gifts? How much charitable giving should be exempt from taxation?

What would it mean for our politics and our economic policies if we structured an economic system from the perspective that every member of humankind is of equal dignity and worth?

What are the most important issues for Christians to consider in developing a political position on law enforcement, crime, and punishment?

A concern for personal safety pervades the citizenry, and, for good reason. Crime rates have increased significantly. Stories of violence dominate newscasts. The concern for crime is real, but fear-based reactions to the crime problem are dangerous.

Hurried attempts to crack down on criminals sometimes lack sound reasoning. Hot in pursuit of safety, legislators fail to consider the consequences of tough anti-crime actions for the maintenance of personal liberties and other social values. A sizable body of law is emerging to address these issues.

Guiding Principles

Solutions for crime do not come easily. At times, basic moral principles get lost amid the fervor of stopping the success of criminals, "leaches on the body politic." Careful thought regarding fundamental principles is needed lest a correction of the crime problem create other, maybe even greater, problems.

Personal Guilt. The Bible declares that we are all sinners; every last one of us. That means we have little to boast about it in relation to each other. Whatever moral one-upsmanship we claim in relation to others is only a matter of degree, not a real distinction. Sooner or later, every one of us takes life into our own hands, a decision that prompts immoral, if not illegal, behavior.

Realistically, we all break the law. Some of us break bigger and more obvious laws than others—from a minor violation of the speed limit in a school zone to a deliberate evasion of the national tax code. Yet, at one time or another, most of us see ourselves as above the law.

Law Enforcement. Maintaining laws to guarantee justice and facilitate an organized society has the endorsement of God. Law enforcement officials do not enjoy a no-holds barred approach to their work, however. Unless officials who administer the law operate by the same standards of justice expected of others, real problems arise.

It's a tough situation. Police must respond to criminal activities with a force that can halt wrongdoing but with a restraint that respects a criminal's rights. Yes, even criminals have rights, as do victims of crimes and police. Violations of the law do not justify an abuse of the violators. Officers of the law live under the same laws they enforce.

Society benefits from an enforcement of law sensitive to the dignity and worth of law enforcement officials, criminals, and victms of criminal acts. Justice must be maintained in a manner that does not erode its foundations.

The ancient image of "blind justice" makes an important point. Laws should be enforced among all citizens equally without regard for racial identity, economic status, religious persuasion, or professional position.

Punishment for What Purpose. Punishment is the consequence of crime. But, punishment toward what end? Or, is punishment an end in itself? People make strong arguments for both views.

On the one hand, punishment is the just dessert for a person who breaks the law. "He had it coming to him." Punishing one person for a crime well may deter others from committing that same crime. Even if not, though, each crime merits punishment.

On the other hand, punishment aims at the rehabilitation of criminals. Lawbreakers are fined severely, incarcerated, or punished in some other manner to bring about a modification in their behavior and to shape them into responsible, contributing members of society.

In reality, these two views of punishment best complement one another rather than compete with each other. In a law-based society, everyone understands that breaking a law means accepting the legally-prescribed punishment for that act. No reason exists, however, for forms of punishment not to be planned and executed to serve a redemptive purpose. Such a view of punishment certainly squares with Christianity's insistence that we never give up on a person.

Holistic Correction. Strict law enforcement and tough penalities for convicted criminals offer little hope for improved conditions apart from significant social changes. Long term solutions to the problem of crime require aggressive actions to deal with the social conditions that breed a criminal mindset—poverty, unemployment, gambling, drug abuse, and lack of education—as well as reacting to criminal behavior. Perhaps the absence of a will to address the causes of crime explains why the United States has more people incarcerated, in numbers and per capita, than any other country in the world.

Security and Freedom. Pervasive fear produces a near psychotic obsession with security. In pursuit of a safe feeling, the public endorses serious infringements on freedom. It's a shortsighted response to lawlessness.

Security that must be purchased by a forfeiture of liberty costs too much. Reckless restrictions on freedom, violations of basic civil rights, and invasions of privacy may net the arrests of a few criminals. In the process, though, distinctions dissolve between those who are breaking the law and those who are keeping the law. Erosions of freedom threaten the security of society to an extent unapproachable by crime.

Political Questions

Affirming general principles related to the problem of crime is far easier than working out the specifics of what these principles mandate as government policy. A political platform requires specific convictions, however.

Rights Issues. Does the Constitution guarantee every citizen a right to own and carry a gun? If so, is protecting this right to bear arms more important than legislating restrictions on sales of handguns and assault weapons in order to save lives?

Should wiretaps be legal when used to entrap suspected criminals or head-off criminal acts? How can the public be protected from an abuse of this investigatory privilege? What restrictions on computer-based communications are you willing to accept? How can an individual's right to privacy be guaranteed without legislation regulating access to certain types of information on the internet?

Does the importance of arresting a lawbreaker outweigh the importance of respecting that person's rights? Is a person still considered innocent until proven guilty, or does society now insist on an individual's guilt as charged until innocence can be proven? What about the rights of victims of crimes? Do we need more legislation on behalf of innocent persons caught up in criminal situations?

Judicial Reform. Does our present judicial system serve the cause of justice? Should we reconsider regulations related to jury trials? Is a unanimous vote by a jury really necessary?

What about the election of judges? Should any person hold a lifetime appointment to the judiciary? Do we need new laws to make the recall of an incompetent judge easier? Should all judges have to be elected to their posts, or should none have to be elected?

Penal Reform. Do I favor the "three strikes and you're out" principle by which a criminal is no longer elgible for release from imprisonment after three offenses? How can we better address the problem of repeat offenders?

Must society address overcrowded prisons characterized by unhealthy living conditions? Or do the comfort and health of prisoners matter? What about treating nonviolent, white collar crimes with less severity than that directed at physically violent offenders?

Are we willing to make a greater financial investment toward programs of rehabilitation within prison communities? Should life sentences be altered when behavior modification seems accomplished? Is capital punishment a just means of society dealing with certain criminals? Given the economic conditions and racial divisions within our society, is capital punishment a racist act of violence on the part of government? Does capital punishment have any value as a deterrent for criminal activities?

What are the most important issues for Christians to consider in developing a political position on environmental concerns?

For Christians, an interest in ecological integrity forms an essential component in moral and political responsibility. A divine mandate to take care of the earth reverberated among the primal sounds of creation. So important is good stewardship in relation to creation, that the apostle Paul labeled as sin any disobedience to this mandated mission from God that resulted in an abuse of the created order—a sin against creation and a sin against God (Rom 8:19-22).

Guiding Principles

Sensitive people attempt to please God by their treatment of creation as well as give praise and thanks to God for the created order. A few guiding principles move thoughtful Christian citizens from an affirmation of basic moral values to an ecological application of these values.

The Priority of Persons. Dignity and worth inhere in personhood—endowments from God, not achievements by individuals. That is why the Bible insists upon the priority of persons individually and communally. Within the global village, need rather than geographical proximity or cultural similarity defines a neighbor. Thus, morally responsible decision-making about environmental concerns must take into consideration an ecological policy's effect upon the people of the land—all the people of all the land.

Rights and Resources. An ancient psalm declares "the earth is the Lord's." As caretakers of God's good earth, we are accountable to God for the manner in which we respect, conserve, and utilize natural resources. Each generation properly draws upon the bounty of the earth for its livelihood, but restraint and preservation are moral imperatives. Every succeeding generation also has a right to enjoy the fruits of creation. A rape of the earth or plunder of its resources is as wrong as harmful violence against persons.

Justice dictates an equitable distribution and consumption of the earth's resources among all peoples. Whether the specific concern is coal, food, timber, or something else, all persons have a right to enjoy its benefits.

Political Questions

Less than thirty years ago, no candidate for the presidency of the nation considered environmental concerns worthy of a major speech. Today, ecological issues pervade political platforms. Like a huge rock dropped into the center of a lake, a commitment to ecological integrity sends waves of interest running in ever-widening circles to lap against distant shores.

Population. Do I favor population control for people or animals, for both or neither? Would I limit the number of children a welfare mother can birth and continue to receive financial aid from the government? What is my view on assisted suicides? Do I recognize euthanasia as a right? What standards would I apply to medical professionals who must make decisions about the use of life-support systems?

Pollution. Do pollution control standards justify the increase in economic expenses required to comply with them? What restrictions should be placed on ocean dumping? How would I balance the need for pollution control over against transportation needs and the interests of manufacturers who produce vehicles for transportation? Do I favor the use of agricultural chemicals that dramatically increase crop production at the expense of burning up the soil over a smaller crop yield based upon fertilizers that do no permanent harm to the soil? Can recycling really solve the problem of waste buildup? If so, should the government make recycling mandatory?

Conservation. Do I support conservation policies related to endangered species? Is the use of chemicals in agriculture a threat to the preservation of plants and trees? Must hunting and fishing restrictions be enforced to guarantee the continuation of wildlife? Would I limit the amount of minerals that can be extracted from the earth during a specific period of time? What conservation regulations for the mining industry would I support?

Energy. What kinds of energy should be legal? Is additional research into the utilization of solar energy worth the cost involved? What about nuclear energy? Do the risks related to it outweigh the benefits of it? Does offshore drilling for new sources of energy constitute a pollution problem? How should we balance the use of cheap energy that dirties the environment and requirements for clean energy that is more expensive? Do all people have a right to energy?

Lifestyle. Should government define personal and familial lifestyle adjustments that are necessary for the conservation of the earth and its resources? Do I favor reduced speed limits on the nation's highways as a means of keeping energy consumption down? Should the government enforce building codes on new construction?

What are the most important issues for Christians to consider in developing a political position on international relations?

Currently, many political leaders are reassessing the United States' role in the world community. Facing a federal budget crunch of extreme proportions and a debilitating national debt, pressure mounts for the nation to turn its focus inward and not worry about the rest of the world. The direction given to international relations impacts almost every other aspect of a political platform.

Guiding Principles

Without question, the people who wrote the Bible took relationships between nations very seriously. Old Testament prophets embraced a vision of international proportions and spoke of God's concern for all nations. Standing firmly in that tradition, Jesus refused confinement by national (as well as cultural and racial) boundaries. True followers of Jesus consider the whole world as their home.

Interdependence. Interdependence in the global community is a spiritual principle as well as a political reality. Even before modern technology and politics brought the nations of the world closer together by means of communication, moral conscientiousness negated a politics of isolation. Biblical morality, in particular, prohibits an individual, an institution, or a nation from functioning as if no one else matters. The nation bears a responsibility in the international community equal to that borne by an individual within the nation. Both are to practice good citizenship.

The Things that Make for Peace. A vision of peace dominates the highest hopes of biblical writers. The things that make for peace always seem to stir political controversy, however.

Amassing public support for a military campaign is relatively easy, though not as easy as in the past. However, gaining a broad-based commitment to expend federal funds for agricultural reform, educational programs, industrial development, and poverty relief in foreign lands is difficult. Yet, expenditures aimed at personal and economic development within nations in crisis represent peacemaking efforts every bit as important as a military mission to halt acts of hostile aggression.

Justice. Justice is an enemy of Christianity wherever it is found—whether in a court room or an office suite, in a legislative proposal or an economic policy, in the consumption of natural resources or the distribution of food. Support for justice transcends national borders.

Widening gaps between the haves and the have-nots and escalating differences between developed nations and developing nations represent grave inequities with serious long-term consequences. A government committed to justice cannot be unconcerned with injustice anywhere. As Jim Wallis wrote, "The circumstances of the most vulnerable among us are always the best test of our human solidarity with one another"[9]—and of our commitment to justice. That principle takes on added importance in a nation that with 6 percent of the world's population consumes 35 percent of the earth's resources.

Political Questions

Correct information is a fundamental component in sound decision-making. Unfortunately, studies demonstrate that public opinions on foreign policy issues in our country suffer from a serious lack of facts.

One recent survey found that 75 percent of the American people believe the United States spends too much money on foreign aid. Of that number, 64 percent want significant cuts in the nation's allocations for foreign aid. Yet, the people surveyed had no idea about the amount of money the nation actually spends on foreign aid. Most estimated an expenditure equal to 15 or 18 percent of the federal budget when the actual cost of foreign aid amounts to less than 1 percent of the federal budget.

Critical cracks appear in political platforms built on flawed data. Asking the right questions is crucial to finding proper answers about foreign policy issues.

Isolationism. The most fundamental issue to be resolved in current foreign aid debates centers on whether or not our nation should adopt an isolationist policy in relation to the rest of the world. To choose a policy of isolationism negates most other foreign relations concerns. An interest in military programs and funding persists. However, considerations of funds for relief efforts, developmental support, and crisis resolution are out of the question. Conversely, rejection of isolationism with a decision to practice international citizenship raises many other questions.

Military Concerns. Is a strong national defense the best guarantee of international peace? Should the nation continue major expenditures for research on new weapons systems? What, if any, parts of the nation's defense budget should be cut in this era of international cooperation?

Should our government pursue further international agreements on disarmament? Are there aspects of disarmament that the nation should initiate unilaterally? Should political officials halt further cutbacks in nuclear warheads?

What is the nation's responsibility in providing military support for international organizations such as the United Nations and the alliance of the North Atlantic Treaty Organization? When participating in a cooperative military campaign, is it appropriate for United States soldiers to take orders from a foreign commander? Should the nation even send military personnel into a foreign situation in which Americans do not have a strategic national interest?

International Police Force. The commitment of United States military troops to serve as an international police force in foreign lands has prompted great controversy in recent years. Both Republican and Democratic administrations have supported such deployments (for example, to Grenada, Haiti, Somalia, and Bosnia). What guidelines should regulate an American military presence for peacekeeping or humanitarian purposes on foreign soil? Should each foreign commitment of personnel be restricted by size and schedule? Should United States troops in peacekeeping situations be allowed to carry loaded weapons with which to retaliate if threatened? Is working for peace among warring factions in another part of the world worth the life of one American soldier?

Aid, Relief, and Empowerment. Our government has a reputation for helping other governments in times of need. Particularly after devastation from a hurricane, an earthquake, a famine, or some other tragedy, our nation sends medical supplies, clothing, and other aid to the affected people. Is this a good use of taxpayers' money? Is it a policy commendable from the perspective of Christian morality?

Should our distribution of food in the international community be contingent upon a government's promises of support for our country? Are we wise to invest United States' funds in education and agricultural development in nations with serious food shortages? Or, should our government leave it to private agencies to address the problem of world hunger?

Is channeling money from our government into support for a young, unstable democracy in another part of the world economically and politically smart? What is the wisdom of enforcing economic blockades around governments of which we disapprove? What about the morality of a blockade that inflicts grave difficulties on innocent citizens without significantly impacting the government authorities of that land?

What are the most important issues for Christians to consider in developing a political position on human rights?

Unlike civil rights, which depend upon guarantees that come with citizenship in a particular government, human rights rest on people's identity as human beings. Human rights precede the provisions of any legal entity and exist without regard for a particular form of government; they are pre-legal and pre-political. No government is justified in abridging the human rights of any person. A political platform devoid of a major emphasis on human rights is unthinkable for a Christian.

Guiding Principles

Faith in the Christ who announced that freeing captives and bringing liberty to the oppressed formed the heart of his mission creates grave concerns about people's rights.

Inalienable Rights. Theologically, human rights derive from the creative activity of God who formed each member of humankind in the *imago Dei* (image of God). God endows every individual with dignity that merits respect and worth that creates rights. Thus, the power of government is limited by the rights that its citizens enjoy by virtue of their identity as persons.

Essential Freedom. People achieve their greatest potential in a context of freedom. Every person has the right to make decisions about political and spiritual beliefs and to act on those beliefs apart from coercion and threats of punishment by a government. Having been made for freedom, people have the right to fully explore that dimension of human nature. To contravene personal freedom is to violate an individual's inalienable right.

The Purpose of Government. Government exists for people, not vice versa. Government best serves society and builds community through providing freedom, maintaining order, and facilitating justice. Fidelity to those essential functions dictates a government's protection of human rights for all of its citizens equally. Arguably, a government that violates the basic human rights of its citizens forfeits its own right to exist.

Political Questions

Most people favor a guarantee of human rights theoretically. Pragmatically, though, debates shroud support for human rights in controversy. Individuals and nations seem unable to agree on what constitutes a human right. Disagreement also arises over the best means for guaranteeing human rights.

Human Rights Abroad. Apparently, the fervor of our nation's support for human rights by other governments is directly proportionate to the "national interests" of the United States at stake in those other governments. Of course, this policy reflects more concern with protecting national interests than with maintaining human rights. Is this a proper basis for our nation's foreign policy on human rights?

The Cost of Protection. Do human rights violations in other nations provide just cause for cutting off foreign aid, revising trade policies, and re-evaluating diplomatic relations with those nations? Should our nation give financial support to governments lax in their support for human rights? An even more controversial question asks whether or not the United States should provide military support on behalf of human rights in foreign governments.

Fundamental Decisions. How important is a guarantee of human rights for all people? Do the risk and potential costs of protecting human rights alter that importance?

Decisions about the definition of rights and the application of that meaning for government policies constitute a major portion of a person's political platform. Ideals have to duke it out with realities. Each rights-related conclusion carries consequences for legislation and budgetary implications.

Has "freedom" become an ugly word?

Liberty generally constitutes the centerpiece around which citizens build their political convictions within a democracy. Christian citizens, specifically, establish freedom as the major criterion for decision-making in the development of a political platform. Freedom has fallen on hard times in the minds of many people, however. The result is a dangerous situation for everyone.

Freedom under Siege

Rising crime rates, violent protests, divisive disagreements over cherished principles, and heated criticisms of organized religion have shaken the security and increased the fears of many citizens. Subsequently, a climate has developed in which serious threats to freedom look and sound like initiatives in the best interest of the health of the nation.

Fear causes shortsightedness and cripples reason. People who are afraid can seldom see past an immediate situation and think through long-term implications of actions aimed at solving a current crisis. Thus, fearful that the nation has lost its moral moorings, people tamper with the principle of religious freedom. Perhaps, so the reasoning (or foolishness) goes, personal fears can be alleviated by mandating that the whole nation pay homage to religion.

Similarly, individuals frightened by an increased potential for crime in their lives support infringements on personal liberties that will give them a greater feeling of security. Anxieties about a malfunctioning criminal justice system cause citizens to downplay the basic concept of "innocent until proven guilty" and flirt with proposals to abandon jury trials. All such attempts to gain immediate relief from fears and anxieties spell potential disaster for the future of liberty.

Freedom is a precious commodity. Efforts to restrict it end up destroying it. There is no such thing as a little bit of freedom. We either have freedom or we don't.

Civil Liberties

Freedom and rights go hand in hand. The United States government perpetuates freedom through guaranteeing constitutionally-based civil rights for all its citizens.

Rights in Question. Rights will always be as controversial as they are essential in a democratic form of government. Endorsing a theory of rights comes easily. Not so a systematic application of a theory of rights to society. Citizens expect the government to ensure fair employment practices. Few, if any, people disagree with protecting a person's right to work and assuring an individual equality in the workplace. Major controversy develops, however, over whether or not work-related rights justify special regulations (a quota system or affirmative action programs, for example) to assure employment opportunities for minorities.

Similarly, social justice receives enthusiastic support. Who can oppose justice in any form? Yet, loud protests greet people's specific claims to a right to food, health care, housing, work, and economic support during retirement when guaranteeing a realization of these rights requires substantive tax increases.

A definition of rights and a projection of how government should guarantee rights in specific social situations constitute a major plank in a person's political platform. Ideals have to duke it out with realities. Every rights-related conclusion carries consequences for legislation and budgetary implications.

The Bill of Rights. Whether or not the Bill of Rights, the first ten amendments to the United States Constitution, could be adopted today remains a serious question. Well-publicized abuses of rights have created an almost paranoid suspicion of rights. Freedom has become a precarious priority within our democracy.

The guarantees of freedom in the First Amendment to the Constitution have been labeled invitations to anarchy and obscenity. Apparently numerous citizens only support the freedom of speech when they find agreeable or tolerable what is said. Some people now want to apply the right to peaceable assembly selectively, providing it for some groups and denying it to others.

Disagreement fails as a valid reason to deny an individual freedom. In fact, freedom's greatest test resides in a person's willingness to protect another person's right to advocate a point of view considered offensive and wrong. If persons with whom we disagree don't enjoy the freedom to speak their minds, print their materials, and assemble with their like-minded friends, ultimately neither do we.

Thankfully, as Edward Tivnan said, the people who invented America

> were not only aware that freedom would breed conflicting values, incomprehension, incoherence, and hostility; they were expecting that such differences would secure the nation's future as a republican democracy.[10]

Religious Liberty

Religious freedom forms the cornerstone for all other freedoms. Many historians consider the principle of religious liberty our nation's greatest contribution to the Western world. Presently, though, even religious freedom faces many detractors.

An Endangered Wall of Separation. Support for the principle of religious freedom resulted in the nation's adoption of the First Amendment to the Constitution. This action gave legal status to two basic provisions: "Congress shall make no law respecting an establishment of religion"—separation of church and state—"or prohibiting the free exercise thereof"—freedom of religion and for religion.

The "no establishment" clause of the Constitution means the government cannot set up an official church or pass laws that aid one religion or all religions. The "free exercise" clause of the Constitution means that government cannot hinder religious activities. Nothing in either of these provisions prohibits healthy interaction between religion and government or seeks to push religion to an isolated periphery of life.

Reflecting on the recently-enacted constitutional guarantee of religious freedom, Thomas Jefferson described the law as "building a wall of separation between Church and State." Almost seventy-five years later, Chief Justice Waite of the United States Supreme Court described Jefferson's metaphor as "an authoritative declaration of the scope and effect of the amendment."[11] Today this historic wall is under a frontal attack.

Religious Right Charges. Some members of the Religious Right directly attack the First Amendment. Keith Fournier from the American Center for Law and Justice likens Jefferson's metaphor of a wall of separation between church and state to communist oppression. Jerry Falwell once labeled the whole church-state principle as "bogus." Other participants in the Religious Right do not attack the First Amendment so much as they lobby for an interpretation of it that rips out its heart and saps it of all strength. David Barton suggests the First Amendment intends to do no more than protect the church from the government. Others claim the first of the Bill of Rights exists only to prevent the nation from establishing a state church.

Judicial Judgments. A careful assessment of the current makeup of the Supreme Court brings to mind the old image of foxes in the chicken house. The very people charged with responsibility for protecting the constitutional principle of religious liberty lean precariously toward a major revision of this principle.

Justices Antonin Scalia and Clarence Thomas along with Chief Justice William H. Rehnquist clearly favor a reversal in major church-state rulings in the past. Rehnquist states his opposition to church-state separation with no reservations:

> The "wall of separation between church and state," is a metaphor based on bad history, a metaphor that has proved useless as a guide to judging. It should be frankly and explicitly abandoned.[12]

So far justices John Paul Stevens, David Souter, and Ruth Bader Ginsburg have voted in support of church-state separation. After a recent split decision (5–4) in which the court permitted government support for religious organization at the University of Virginia, Justice Souter voiced his alarm: "The Court, today, for the first time, approves direct funding of core religious activities by an arm of the state."[13]

Justices Stephen G. Breyer—the newest member of the court—Sandra Day O'Connor, and Anthony M. Kennedy cannot be positioned on church-state separation. Though Kennedy and O'Connor have not endorsed the revisionist position of three of their colleagues, they have expressed concerns over the high court's past rulings.

Legislative Actions. Speaker of the House of Representatives Newt Gingrich requested Congressman Ernest Istook to lead a task force on legislation to overturn Supreme Court decisions prohibiting prayer in public schools. Simultaneously, the Majority Leader in the House of Representatives has made clear his intention to pass an educational reform package that includes vouchers for the support of private education. *Cause for Concern.* I am no alarmist, but I see the principle of religious liberty in real trouble. Relentless powerful attacks on church-state separation continue. The historic wall of separation desperately needs reinforcement and broad-based support from the millions of American citizens who have enjoyed its benefits through the years.

Three Critical Issues. Ironically, the most serious threats to religious freedom and church-state separation in our nation today come from various segments of the religious community, not from the government. Three initiatives form a sharp-edged blade on a bulldozer rumbling toward the demolition of the historic wall of church-state separation.

Mandated Religious Exercises. When Newt Gingrich, a Republican from Georgia, assumed the position of Speaker of the House of Representatives in January 1995, he immediately promised a vote on a prayer-in-public-schools constitutional amendment by the following Fourth of July. Fortunately, it didn't happen. Conservative Christian politicians discovered the difficulties involved in an attempt to legislate religious exercises for public settings. Gary Bauer observed, "If you get ten legal scholars in a room to talk about this (a prayer amendment), you get eleven different opinions."[14]

No legislation or constitutional amendment to provide for prayer is needed. The Supreme Court's famous "no prayer in schools" decision in 1962—perhaps the most misunderstood and misinterpreted legal decision in history—struck down only state-written, teacher-led prayers in public classrooms. By a vote of 6 to 1, the justices ruled that students' repetition of a "non-sectarian" prayer composed by the New York Board of Regents unconstitutionally involved the government in a religious practice. The high court officials explained,

> It is no part of the business of government to compose official prayers for any group of the American people to recite as a part of a religious program carried on by government.[15]

Theologically and pragmatically, prayer never can be eliminated by anyone anywhere for any reason. Prayer is a personal religious act

that can be practiced as meaningfully (if not more so) in private silence as in public pronouncements.
Tax Dollars for Private Education. Most popular among present plans for parochial aid is some form of voucher system. Parents could pay for their child's enrollment in a private school using a voucher that the educational institution would redeem for cash from a government treasury.

Supporters of vouchers describe their interests as providing parents a choice in educational institutions for their children and eliminating double taxation for people who choose private schools. Choice already exists, however. The tuition required to enroll in a private school is not a tax. Enactment of a voucher system of education would allow institutions to underwrite religious indoctrination with public money—a critical broadside against the historic wall of church-state separation.

Private religious schools account for 85 percent of the total private school enrollment in the nation. Additionally, a voucher system likely would spell the demise of public education, a dangerous development in a democratic society. Though advocates of vouchers argue that competition in education will improve public schools, not a shred of evidence is available to support this claim.

Despite the Christian Coalition's strong support for vouchers, voters have rejected vouchers in California, Oregon, and Colorado. In thirteen other states, voucher proposals did not even get through the state legislatures. Only Wisconsin and Ohio have passed legislation supportive of vouchers. Both programs are under legal challenge in the courts. No state or federal court has ever upheld the use of vouchers to support education in private religious schools.

A Religious Equality Amendment. In its "Contract with the American Family," the Christian Coalition assigned top priority to securing the adoption of an amendment to the Constitution to guarantee a free expression of religion in all public places. Great enthusiasm for the adoption of this amendment, however, did not translate into a quick drafting of it. Conservative religious leaders experienced grave difficulties in finding terminology acceptable to all parties involved.

After months of debate and dialogue on the text of the amendment, two proposals were introduced to Congress in November

1995—one by Representative Istook (R–OK) and the other by Representative Hyde (R–IL). The following month, Senator Hatch (R–IL) introduced into the Senate a bill similar to the one Hyde placed before the House of Representatives. Both proposed amendments look simple, innocent, and general at first glance. However, each opens the door to a whole new constitutional perspective on religious freedom and church-state separation.

Each amendment authorizes equal amounts of government funding to be distributed between parochial schools and public schools as well as between churches and secular charitable institutions. Can you imagine the economic impact of this provision on the federal government, not to mention its damage to public education and to church-state relations? Though the proposed amendment's emphasis on equality between religious and secular activities has not been fully explored, the special exemptions that religion receives under current law likely would be abolished. What's more, no clear understanding exists about the amendment's emphasis on religious expressions among private individuals or groups.

Would a student praying over a school's intercom system represent a private person with freedom to pray aloud without discrimination? Would schools be required to allow students to pray aloud whenever and wherever they so desired and to offer any kind of prayer they wished, including prayers prepared for them by religious officials?

The Religious Equality Amendment is not needed. Consequences of this act would actually hurt religion more than help it. With government funding comes government control. With government's acknowledgment of religion comes government's choice of which religion to acknowledge. Though billed as a means of clarifying the First Amendment, in the long run this amendment would gut the First Amendment. Government would be worse off, and religion would suffer even more.

Notes

[1]A concise presentation of the thoughts of this great church-state scholar can be found in Franklin Hamlin Littell, *From State Church to Pluralism: A Protestant Interpretation of Religion in American History* (Garden City NJ: Anchor Books, Doubleday & Company, Inc., 1962).

[2]Bruce C. Birch and Larry L. Rasmussen, *Bible and Ethics in the Christian Life* (Minneapolis MN: Augsburg, 1976) 135.

[3]Roland H. Bainton, *Christian Attitudes Toward War and Peace: A Historical Survey and Critical Re-evaluation* (New York: Abingdon, 1960) 71.

[4]Ibid., 73.

[5]Jim Wallis, *The Soul of Politics: A Practical and Prophetic Vision for Change* (New York: The New Press and Orbis Books, 1994) 15.

[6]William Temple, *Christianity & Social Order* (New York: Seabury, 1977) 67.

[7]John C. Bennett, *Christian Ethics and Social Policy* (New York: Charles Scribner's Sons, 1946) 77.

[8]Robert Benne, "Capitalism," *The Westminster Dictionary of Christian Ethics*, eds. James F. Childress and John Macquarrie (Philadelphia: Westminster, 1986) 75.

[9]Wallis, 71.

[10]Edward Tivnan, *The Moral Dilemma: Confronting the Ethical Issues of Our Day* (New York: Simon & Schuster, 1995) 247.

[11]Charles C. Haynes, *Religion in American History: What to Teach and How* (Alexandria VA: Association for Supervision and Curriculum Development, 1990) 53.

[12]Robert Boston, *Why the Religious Right is Wrong about Separation of Church & State* (Buffalo NY: Prometheus, 1993) 74.

[13]Linda Greenhouse, "Church-State Ties: Court Rules University Must Help Subsidize Religious Journal," *The New York Times*, 30 June 1995, A1, A24.

[14]Tony Mauro, "Amendment on School Prayer on Slow Track," *USA Today*, 15 May 1995.

[15]*Engel v. Vitale*, 370 U.S. 421 (1962), cited in Boston, 103.

Part III

FAITH
—*and*—
POLITICS

Questioning for Whom to Vote

Notes from a Personal Pilgrimage

My first foray into political campaigns came during the summer of my tenth year. I volunteered to work for Frank Clement who was running for governor in my home state of Tennessee. Over the course of several weeks, I sealed envelopes, visited door-to-door in various neighborhoods passing out literature, distributed lapel buttons, and worked at various other chores to support the candidacy of Frank Clement.

Why Clement? I really don't know. I'm sure parental influence played a role. What I remember most, though, was the man's charisma. Every time I listened to Clement speak, I thought he was the best speaker I had ever heard. Besides, he quoted the Bible a lot. I really liked that—a sign that my candidate was a deeply religious man, I thought.

Criticisms of my gubernatorial candidate caught me off guard. How could anyone not like this man? With stunned dismay, I listened to some of my friends accuse my candidate of holding the Bible in one hand and a liquor bottle in the other. Where I lived, that was about the worst charge that could be made against a person. A question nagged at me, "Am I doing wrong in working for this man?"

Whether or not I ever conscientiously answered that question, I don't know. But, I didn't stop campaigning for the man. And, Clement was elected governor of Tennessee. What great excitement! In a childish manner, I was convinced that I had played an important role in the new governor's ascendancy to the state capital.

Other than appreciating the candidate's regular citations of the Scriptures, I supported Frank Clement primarily because of his charisma—a captivating blend of attractive personality, commanding appearance, and powerful rhetoric. Clement's positions on issues were inconsequential to me. At that point in my life, I could not even have defined the meaning of a political platform much less described the one on which my candidate ran for office.

Putting Away Childish Things

The reasons a ten-year-old supports a candidate for public office should differ substantially from a rationale for political allegiances among adults. The real tests of governmental leadership revolve around a politician's prioritizing of issues, aggressiveness in policy initiatives, and support for legislative programs—not rhetoric and appearance. Good decisions about whom to support in an election require knowing more about a candidate than how many times she quotes from the Bible, how he looks on television, and the emotion with which she speaks.

Eventually I learned that support for a candidate's bid for a public office based on a single issue is as dangerous as support generated by cosmetic reasons. This truth registered with me most powerfully during an electoral campaign in which a friend of mine urged me to support a mayoral candidate who was a member of the congregation of which he was pastor. That request seemed reasonable enough. Besides, as a Baptist, I felt good about being able to vote for another Baptist.

When I began to compare this particular candidate's views on government with those of his opponent, my thinking quickly changed. I realized that because one candidate and I shared a common loyalty to a Baptist church was no reason for me to vote for him as mayor. What mattered in the mayoral election were the candidates' positions on city taxes, public education, cooperation with county officials, and a host of other issues. When it came to deciding about who would make a good mayor, a candidate's religious affiliation was not nearly so important as his political platform.

A Turning Point

Within the past twenty years, no event raised the political hopes of religious people like the election of James Earl Carter to the presidency of the United States. Ironically, this same event quickly became a lightning rod bombarded by criticisms from many evangelical Christians. Fundamentalist religious leaders used Carter's presidency as an incentive for sounding alarms regarding Christians and politics. They parlayed negative views of Carter's administration into a launching pad for the Religious Right.

In the beginning, all was well. Jimmy Carter's campaign for the national presidency gave a tremendous boost to conservative Christians' involvement in politics. Throughout his pursuit of the highest office in the land, Carter unashamedly spoke of his identity, beliefs, and ministry as a "born again" Christian. Hopes soared. When Carter won the election, elated Christians rejoiced. An evangelical Christian, one of us, now occupied the Oval Office, the most powerful political position in the free world.

Euphoria quickly dissipated, however. High-flying hopes among evangelical Christians took a nose-dive and hit the ground with a thud. Conservative religious voters found Carter's "born again" Christianity insufficient to counterbalance their opposition to many of his specific policies. Some disappointed people in this emerging religio-political power bloc decided that President Carter was not even a Christian. Interestingly, their judgment rested on Carter's conformity (or lack of it) to their assumptions on a variety of political issues, not on the basis of his Christian confession or witness to religious truths.

The rapidity with which support for the president turned into hostile opposition alarmed me. I found myself struggling with a number of pressing questions about Christians' support for a particular candidate for public office.

Voting for Satan

A few weeks prior to the 1992 presidential election, a political ad in the Saturday morning edition of a local newspaper caught my eye. In the religion section of the paper, blocked and printed in heavy black ink, the message read, "Choose: Clinton or Christianity. Keep America Strong!" The advertisement was paid for by an organization called "Christians Against Clinton."[1]

What a relief it would be if deciding about for whom to vote in a presidential election, or any in election, could be simplified to that extent! Christian citizens would be spared the task of reading through position papers, evaluating campaign promises, and studying the credentials of various candidates. Knowing that a vote for one candidate represents support for Christianity and the strengthening of America while a vote for another candidate signals opposition to both and ultimately a vote for Satan, how easy it would be for Christians to pull the lever in a voting machine. But it's not that easy—not by a long shot.

While pondering that extremist political advertisement, a number of old questions linked up with several new ones. How should a Christian decide about which candidate to support in an election?

How much importance should be assigned to a candidate's religious convictions in considering that person's suitability for an office? If an individual's confession of faith is considered of little consequence, what is important? What qualifications for public office bear the most significance to Christian voters? What do people of faith need to know about candidates for whom they vote? These questions, and many more, persist.

What do you know about the candidate personally?

The electorate properly displays great interest in a candidate's age, family background, education, and work experience. Though no one of these personal factors is likely to determine a voter's decision about a candidate, all of this data can be instructive.

Vita

Opinions differ dramatically about the importance of various line items in a candidate's personal résumé. Some voters fear youth, while others look with disfavor on a politician of advanced age. One voter likes a candidate who comes from a family historically aligned with politics, while another vows never to vote again for an old-line family politician. Some people find a candidate with no previous political experience attractive, while others decry a lack of experience in government as a debilitating weakness.

Differences of opinion also cluster around the significance of other data on a candidate's vita—educational institutions attended, academic degrees earned, marital status, military service or lack of it, and various awards and honors received. A discernible pattern on a candidate's biographical data sheet may serve as the decisive factor in a voter's decision about that candidate.

Health

What about a candidate's health? That is a terribly important question. Be careful, though, about how much weight gets assigned to its answer. Realistically, some politicians function more effectively despite their struggles with ill health than do others who enjoy perfectly good health.

During the 1992 presidential election, the electronic media made a big deal of George Bush's upset stomach during a state dinner in Japan. Come on! People who run for public office—even the presidency of the United States—are individuals just like the rest of us.

They have good days and bad days, experience moments of exhilaration and fight the lure of depression, develop upset stomachs when badly fatigued or when their system fails to properly digest a particular food—in other words, they get sick and get well just like other people. A candidate cannot be more than a human being. Disappointment and anxieties will be constant companions of expectations to the contrary.

Image

Mass communications feed the public's insatiable appetite for personal information on highly visible candidates in electoral campaigns. Television especially provides citizens a means to see a politician up close. Honestly, though, what first appears as a blessing may later take on the nature of a curse. Aware of the public's interest in personal factors, many candidates use the media to create an image of themselves that may have little relationship to reality.

A preoccupation with image prompts more interest in looks and sounds than in political substance. Thus, candidates' made-for-television political advertisements reflect far more concern for flattering camera angles, winsome facial expressions, and memorable sound bites than for a serious articulation of political vision and an honest introduction to a person.

Image is not everything. Perception is not reality. The better voters get to know a candidate as a person and a politician, the more likely they are to make a responsible electoral decision.

Experience

If a candidate has served previousy in a political office, the record of that tenure can enlighten voters. How did the person perform in the prior position of service? Was the candidate faithfully present when meetings were held, reports given, and votes taken? Did the candidate demonstrate a conscientious approach to political decision-making? Could the candidate build coalitions and bring diverse groups together in support of important goals? What strengs became apparent during her time in office? What about the weaknesses that showed up? How were the politician's rapport with the public and relations with the media?

Knowledge about a candidate's support, or lack of it, in his home-town or native state provides particularly helpful information. What other elections, if any, has this candidate entered? How did he fare? Why did he win or lose? A previous record of experience makes knowing a candidate eas-ier. That is not to suggest, however, that prior experience in public service should be a prerequisite for a person to run for an elected office. In some instances, beginners bring to their responsibilities an energy, objectivity, and creativity missing among political veterans. Always interesting to find out about a first-time candidate, though, is her answer to the question, "Why are you running for public office, particularly this one?"

Now a caveat. When a candidate seeks the nation's presidency, a state's governorship, or an executive-level post in a municipal govern-ment, professional experience that contributes to competence to do the job is a serious concern. A total absence of experience in critical decision-making and leadership responsibilities raises serious doubts about a candidate's potential for effectiveness in an executive office.

Is a "liberal" candidate dangerous? What about a "conservative"?

Potentially beneficial discussions of various politicians frequently get short-circuited by the labels "conservative" and "liberal." Advocates of competing political philosophies have turned these historically helpful terms into divisive stereotypes.

In the present political climate, most candidates for public office scramble to adorn themselves with the mantel of conservatism, avoid-ing the tag of "liberal" like a plague. Popular perceptions associate a "conservative" with good, cautious, righteous, and wise leadership dedicated to security. Conversely, caricatures depict a "liberal" as reck-less, generous to a fault, and innovative to the point of jeopardizing security. Such stereotypes ignore history and hinder the dialogue of progress by fueling needless debates that are as regressive as they are fiery.

A Brief History Lesson

The word "conservative" derives from a root referring to weapons or armor designed to protect a person from change or destruction. Thus, a "conservative" distrusts attempts at change and favors preservation of the established order. The term "liberal" comes from a root meaning to grow. Predictably, then, a "liberal" supports change for the sake of progress and rejects the argument that tradition or orthodoxy should impede progress.

Conservatives and liberals worked together in the birthing of the United States of America. Against the best judgments of conservatives, liberals began the push for freedom from England. While liberals called for revolution, conservatives argued in favor of order and stability. Thus, the Declaration of Independence is a liberal document.

As a new government took shape, liberal politicians advocated strong guarantees of political, religious, and economic freedom. Patriots such as Thomas Paine and Thomas Jefferson pleaded for governmental structures to protect individual liberties and allow persons to develop their powers to their fullest potential—a "Bill of Rights." However, conservatives prevailed in writing the Constitution of the United States, at least initially.

A Dramatic Flip-Flop

Originally, unlike conservatives who pushed for a powerful government of large proportions, liberal politicians wanted a limited government. Once a participatory democracy developed, however, a dramatic flip-flop occurred. Today citizens associate large government with the political philosophy of liberals and a limited government with the political goal of conservatives.

So, how can conservatives and liberals be identified? A person's posture toward change remains the major criterion by which to determine this distinction. Even this obvious standard of judgment, though, is no longer easily applied.

In the United States, conservatives could be expected to preserve, or conserve, the Constitution; and liberals to ignore, alter, or move beyond the Constitution. Presently, though, major shifts are negating these classic expectations. Liberals now argue for a maintenance of the

Constitution—a conservative position—while conservatives advocate major amendments to the Constitution. Persons labeled as liberals defend the Constitution's sufficiency to provide for the nation's needs—a conservative point of view. On the other hand, conservatives—both self-declared and publicly recognized—push for constitutional amendments aimed at outlawing abortion, establishing religious practices in public places, and mandating the adoption of a balanced federal budget—liberal policies.

Needed: Cooperation not Corruption

Historically, American patriots have appreciated both conservative and liberal politicians. No good reason exists for either "liberal" or "conservative" to become a pejorative label. Our government has functioned best when liberals and conservatives regularly engaged in controversial but cooperative debates with each other.

Liberals believe strongly in individual rights and social improvement. They see no problem in people disagreeing with each other, even opposing liberalism. In fact, they encourage resistance and debate. True to this spirit, liberals feel no hesitancy about acknowledging their errors.

Conservatives tend to be more staunch. They believe that being right (orthodox, politically correct) is more important than protecting rights (liberties). Consequently, conservatives do not welcome disagreements or deal gracefully with mistakes. Any deviation from the conservative standard in ideology and action is wrong and in need of correction.

These two attitudes often result in conflict. Liberals view conservatives' commitment to orthodoxy and insistence on agreement as autocratic, fanatical, or fascist. Conservatives see liberals' openness to new ideas and tolerance for different viewpoints as dangerous indifference indicative of a lack of moral standards. At their best, each disagrees with the other but allows the other the right to participate in governing the nation. At their worst, each translates opposition to ideology into a justification for excluding the other from political dialogue. Extremism hastens a worst-case scenario.

Extreme conservatives become so passionately committed to a particular program or policy that they no longer trust the democratic process. While tirelessly trying to subvert governmental procedures to accomplish their partisan purposes, such conservatives angrily denounce all who oppose their efforts. Likewise, extremist liberals disdain the kind of dialogue that they normally welcome, seek to manipulate decision-makers whose actions they usually respect, and look down their political noses at all who disagree with them. Our government now, as in the past, needs input from both conservatives and liberals. Vigilantly fighting the corruption of extremism, Christian citizens do well to listen and learn from both liberals and conservatives; ignoring stereotypes about them, learning from the substance of their words and deeds, and joining their campaigns.

Isn't it good for a candidate to promise to rise above politics?

"Politics" is a morally neutral term, a means of decision-making and governance that can be utilized for either good or bad purposes. Politics is the way civil government in the United States works. The whole business of debating ideological positions, building a power base, consolidating support, exerting personal influence, forming alliances, and working out compromises is politics—all that and more. Politics is how legislation gets passed, policies established, budgets adopted and funded, appointments made, and candidates elected to public office.

Occasionally I hear someone derisively say of people in government, "They're all just a bunch of politicians." Well of course, they are. What else did we expect? Politics is the art of government. The people who offer leadership in our government better be politicians—good politicians.

A candidate for political office who disdains politics faces a fate similar to that of an athlete who despises competition or a chef who dislikes both food and cooking. A person who does not know how to listen to opposing points of view, establish trust, make concessions, build consensus, adjust directions, and keep in touch with the electorate best not run for office. If elected, though, that individual will be miserable personally and a failure professionally.

Unfortunately, a politician's loud disclaimer of political action while seeking election to a political office usually represents little more than a rhetorical propaganda device. Amid a relentless search for supportive votes, a candidate tries to elevate her public persona by suggesting that, unlike other candidates for political offices, she can do a political job without doing politics. That very indication is itself a political strategy, though a very poor one.

Does a candidate's political affiliation really matter?

The importance of a candidate's political affiliation increases in direct proportion to the level of government in which that candidate seeks an office. Local elections for city council members, county judges, members of a police jury, mayors, and school board members highlight an array of issues that overshadow candidates' choices of a political party. At the state level, party affiliation makes a bigger difference. Gubernatorial candidates and individuals seeking seats in state legislatures value party endorsements for a political identification of their philosophies as well as for financial support in their campaigns. In national politics, party affiliations mean everything—from qualifying a candidate to seek election to a particular office to identifying that candidate's political persuasions.

We only vote for a particular man or woman in an election, but along with the winner of an election comes the winner's political party, like it or not.

What's the Difference Between Democrats and Republicans?

Significant differences in philosophies, priorities, and programs distinguish the two major political parties in the United States from each other. Generally speaking, Republicans prize individual initiative and a major role for local governments, while Democrats favor more responsibilities for the federal government in directing people's affairs. Republicans tend to be oriented to the interests of the white-collar business community, while Democrats identify more with blue-collar laborers. Citizens usually equate Democrats with "big government" and Republicans with a smaller federal government.

Platforms. A quick look at the 1992 political platform of each major party documents their clearly-defined differences.[2] More than ever before, the Republican platform bore the unmistakable imprint of the Religious Right's growing influence in its ranks. Here is a sampling of immediately obvious distinctions between the parties:

Priorities. Republicans made the family their number-one priority: "Our national renewal starts with the family." Democrats gave first place in their platform to the economy: "Democrats in 1992 hold nothing more important for America than an economy that offers growth and jobs for all."

Education. Republicans favored the possibility of federal financial support for private education: "Parents have the right to choose the best school for their children." Democrats endorsed the importance of public education and opposed parochial aid: "We oppose . . . efforts to bankrupt the public school system . . . through private school vouchers."

Health Care. Republicans called for health care choices to remain in the hands of individual citizens: "Republicans believe government control of health care is irresponsible and ineffective." Democrats advocated major health care reform: "All Americans should have universal access to quality, affordable health care—not as a privilege, but as a right."

Civil Rights. Republicans renewed their commitment to women's rights, reaffirmed support for the right of an unborn child, and defended people's constitutional right to bear arms. Democrats affirmed women's rights, including every woman's right to make an individual decision about abortion, and advocated a shutdown in "weapons bazaars."

Welfare. Republicans called for major welfare reform: "Welfare is the enemy of opportunity and a stable family." Democrats also supported welfare reform: "Welfare should be a second choice, not a way of life."

Government. Republicans favored decentralized authority and self-government, vowing to "concentrate power in town halls and the American home." Democrats promised a more flexible federal government "that improves services, expands choices, and empowers citizens and communities to change our country from the bottom up."

Candidates. Wise decisions about candidates should take into consideration answers to a few basic questions about their party affiliations: Has this man always been a member of the same political party? If not, why did he change? Does this woman's campaign promises square with the political platform of her party? If not, why is she deviating from her party's positions? What is the strength of a party's support for the candidate running under its banner?

Which Party Is Most Christian?

Even phrasing the above question makes me uncomfortable. It conjures up memories of the mind-set that paid for the newspaper ad, "Choose Clinton or Christianity." Obviously, though, other people have no problem with either the question or its answer. Jerry Falwell has asserted that at the present time the Republican Party is the best repository of Judeo-Christian morality on the political scene. Conversely, a friend of mine explains that he "always just votes with Jesus—as a Democrat." My friend was joking. Falwell was serious.

Historic Christian values can be found in both major political parties in the United States. To view either of these organizations as a prime repository of Christian morality, however, is a serious mistake. The church—the corporate body of Christians and local expressions of the body of Christ—has enough trouble representing Christian values. And an accurate presentation of Christian truth forms the heart of its divinely-ordained mission. Why, then, would anyone even look to a political party for a presentation of Christian values when its primary goal is winning elections to serve the nation, not bearing witness to a particular religion?

Switching Parties

Changing political party affiliation has become an increasingly popular phenomenon. Since the 1992 election, several major politicians have renounced their Democratic identity to join the GOP. Some of these switches can be explained by a desire to go with a winner. A major power shift in the United States Congress has caused politicians who lost power to desire to identify with the majority again. Other transfers represent the shifting political values associated with historic parties. Conservative Democrats now look more like traditional Republicans, and more progressive Republicans appear in the tradition associated with previously moderate Democrats. When voting for a candidate who has changed parties, knowledge of why the change took place is helpful information. Did the politician renounce all his old party's convictions or change loyalties on the basis of one or two policies of importance to her? Does the candidate have sufficient status in his newly selected party to work effectively with his colleagues?

What about Independents?

Persons who seek political office as Independents face an uphill struggle. In national elections, Independents encounter near insurmountable problems both as realities during a campaign and as prospects if elected. In some states, even getting on a ballot as an Independent is a difficult task.

Independent candidates significantly impact the outcome of national and local political campaigns, however, as did Ross Perot in 1992. Though Independent candidates often lose elections, their presence on a ballot has a direct bearing on the outcome of those elections. Not infrequently, the political fortunes of the other candidates well could have been reversed had not an Independent redistributed the public's votes on election day.

Independents experience special problems caused by a lack of financing from a national party and an absence of time-tested local party networks to build support. Additionally, citizens tend to suspicion an Independent's ability to work within a two-party system of government if elected to office.

Candidates who run on an Independent ticket require special attention. A wise voter wants to know why this candidate is running as an Independent. Did he take on the Independent identity because he lost the backing of his party and wanted to continue campaigning? Did she get angry at her party and withdraw from it because of major differences of opinion? Or, is this person a thorough-going Independent unwilling to relate to either major party?

Whose Pocketbook Is Showing?

Voters can learn a great deal about the strength of a candidate's party affiliation and the breadth of her political loyalties by discovering whose money finances her campaign. Contributions from special interest groups attract particular attention. Knowledge of the sources of a candidate's financial support provides insights into the candidate's friends and persons to whom the candidate is politically indebted.

For example, a candidate heavily endowed with campaign contributions from the National Rifle Association is not likely to favor gun control. Candidates with substantive support from the defense industry can be expected to protect their self-interests as well as to act on behalf of the good of the nation. Is the candidate heavily supported by mainline party members or by persons seeking special political favors?

How important is a candidate's confession of religious beliefs?

Article VI of the United States Constitution prohibits religious tests as a qualification for public office. Accordingly, a candidate's religious confession should not be a factor in an election. Presently, though, numerous organizations oppose this constitutional provision (in practice if not in theory) as they work to elect only "good Christians" to serve in political offices.

Articulating the point of view of rabid religionists, David Barton told the 1994 annual conference of the Christian Coalition, "If the nation's going to be blessed, it's because the righteous rule," and "The righteous have to elect 'em."[3]

What's in a Word?

Obviously the religious persuasion of a political candidate means a great deal to a large number of voters. Strangely, though, candidates' public statements of their religious convictions carry minimal significance amid the heat of a political campaign. Not even members of the Religious Right assign much importance to a candidate's personal confession of faith. At the national level particularly, a candidate's party affiliation and political platform carry far more weight with voters than his or her declarations of religious beliefs.

In the national presidential election of 1980, the religious convictions and practices of the two major candidates contrasted sharply. Jimmy Carter identified with conservative evangelical Christians as he described his "born again" experience of Christian faith. Ronald Reagan talked of the importance of religious faith only in general, if not vague, terms. Carter regularly participated in congregational worship, prayed in public, supported a local church with his presence and resources, and refused to serve alcoholic beverages at many political events. Reagan did not make a practice of attending congregational worship services and even kept his charitable contributions proportionately small. Yet, conservative Christians enthusiastically endorsed Ronald Reagan as their presidential candidate. One conservative Christian commented about so many of his colleagues endorsing Ronald Reagan:

> By 1984, it was inconceivable that these churchmen could have mistaken Reagan's patent lack of personal interest in things religious for a deep commitment of faith . . . Reagan became God's candidate because he was, in their view, politically correct.[4]

Another anomaly developed in the presidential election of 1992. Religious conservatives bitterly opposed the candidacy of Bill Clinton, a longtime member of a conservative, Christian, evangelical church, to support George Bush whose religious language, thought, and affiliation were far removed from conservative Christianity. For members of the Religious Right, the personal confessions of religious belief made by Bush and Clinton paled in significance beside their political views.

That's perfectly alright. In fact, it's the way things should be. A candidate's religious confession should not be a voter's primary concern in the election of a president. However, campaigners wrongly turned a deaf ear to competing candidates' personal statements of religious belief and then, on the basis of political (not religious) convictions, lauded one candidate as more religious than the other.

Religionists need make no apology for deciding their support for a candidate on the basis of that person's political platform, but they have no reason for seeking to camouflage such a choice under the rubric of religion. Honesty remains the best policy.

So, what's in a word? Writers of the United States Constitution got it right the first time: no religious confession should be used as a criterion for determining a candidate's qualification to hold a public office.

When Religion Matters

The Constitution does not eliminate religion from voters' concerns; it only prohibits personal confessions of faith from disqualifying candidates for public offices. Religion remains a part of the mix that informs voters' decisions about candidates who merit support.

Denominational Affiliation. When John F. Kennedy received the Democratic nomination for president in 1960, evangelical Protestants cried, "Foul!" Well-intentioned people warned that as a devotee of the Roman Catholic Church, Kennedy, if elected president, would be obligated to take his orders from the Pope in Rome rather than from the United States Constitution or the American people. Scores of people argued that Kennedy's religious preference should disqualify him as a candidate for the national presidency. W. A. Criswell, pastor of the largest Southern Baptist church in the nation, predicted that Kennedy's election would spell the death of a free church in a free state.

In that election, concerns about a candidate's religion mattered for good reasons (political as well as religious reasons). Though a Roman Catholic had been nominated for the presidency as early as 1928, the issue of a Catholic president's allegiance to Rome never had been adequately addressed. Rank prejudices stirred unfounded fears, particularly among conservative Christians. Concerned citizens demanded to know the role that candidate Kennedy's religious affiliation would play in his leadership of the nation, if elected president.

Fortunately, Kennedy addressed the issue straightforwardly:

> Whatever one's religion in his private life may be, for the office-holder, nothing takes precedence over his oath to uphold the Constitution and all its parts—including the First Amendment and the strict separation of church and state.[5]

The flip side of the Catholic-Protestant religious affiliation issue arose during the 1976 campaign for the presidency. A leading Roman Catholic, Andrew Greeley, warned fellow Catholics that they should fear the Carter-Mondale ticket because of Carter's roots in an anti-Catholic tradition.

John Kennedy voiced a principle regarding a candidate's denominational affiliation that should be the standard for office-seekers and a criterion for judgment among voters. Kennedy said,

> I believe in America . . . where no Catholic prelate would tell the president (should he be Catholic) how to act, and no Protestant minister would tell his parishioners for whom to vote—where no church or church school is granted any public funds or political preference—and where no man is denied public office merely because his religion differs from the president who might appoint him or the people who might elect him. . . . where religious liberty is so indivisible that an act against one church is treated as an act against all.[6]

Religious Convictions. Some historians judge that Kennedy's election to the White House ended the public's concern about a candidate's religion. Not so. The issue is alive and well (or sick) today. The scope of its concern has broadened considerably, however—from religious affiliations to religious convictions. Many citizens now fear the influence of fundamentalist religion on a candidate for public office as gravely as earlier evangelicals feared the impact of Kennedy's catholicism.

Certain types of questions about a candidate's religious convictions merit attention and answers. Voters cannot afford to ignore a would-be public official's religion-based affirmation of white-supremacy or anti-Semitism. What about a candidate for a national office whose interpretation of biblical prophecy dictates special privileges for the state of Israel? Are the best interests of the government served by people who practice a doomsday ecology or an Armageddon-oriented approach to national defense? And, what about a candidate who seeks a political position as a power base for launching an evangelical crusade?

Conclusion

A candidate's confession of religious beliefs provides important information for voters to consider alongside many other factors related to

that person's potential for public service. A candidate's church affiliation and personal theology should be of little consequence to the
electorate, however. What matters most is the candidate's position on
issues that impact the religious practices (or lack of them) among all
the citizens of the nation.

Once a person accepts responsibility as a public official, that indi-
vidual takes on a solemn obligation to foster a democratic form of
government as provided in the Constitution of the United States.
Acting as a government leader, a person functions not so much as a
Jew, an atheist, an evangelical Christian, an agnostic, or a Roman
Catholic but as an American.

What about the issue of character?
Should voters consider a candidate's personal character?

Character issues have vaulted to the forefront of political discussions
in recent elections. At every level of government, politicians seeking
office have had to drop out of campaigns because of negative public
reactions to disclosures about their personal character.

A strong interest in personal moral integrity merits commendation.
Take care, though. Hypocrisy runs rampant. Under the guise of an
interest in good character, ethical issues can be manipulated to serve
partisan political purposes.

A Nebulous Issue

Character describes that quality in a person that allows her to stand up,
alone if necessary, and defend the values of greatest importance in her
life. By definition, character rests on assumptions. However, disagreements over which assumptions produce differences of opinion on what
constitutes character. A courageous display of personal convictions in
the face of harsh criticism looks like strong character to some people.
The same behavior appears to other folks—those who disagree with
the acted-out convictions—like an arrogant display of evil, an indication of questionable character.

What determines "good character?" Answers to that question usually focus on personal traits. These traits may be as general as doing
right and avoiding wrong. Or, the concept of good character may take

shape around specifics—a practice of the four "cardinal virtues" (prudence or practical wisdom, justice, temperance, and fortitude or courage) and abstinence from the seven "deadly sins" (pride, sloth, envy, anger, avarice, gluttony, and lust).

Personal Sins and Political Service

Monumental changes have occurred in the way character issues impact an election. For many years, media personnel considered the private lives of public officials no one else's business. Reporters never made even well-known character flaws among individuals at the highest level of government a part of the public record. No more. Presently, even an inaccurate rumor about an immoral act can be reported as a major news story that ruins a politician's chances for election or re-election.

The new situation raises serious questions about the relationship between the reality of personal wrongdoing and a capacity for effective political service in an individual's life. Is advocacy for a particular moral principle (by words or example) the responsibility of a public official? In what manner does private ethical behavior influence a person's potential for effective political service? Does the public have a right to know the personal morals of every candidate who seeks a public office? Do media representatives have an obligation (moral or professional) to report incidents of private misbehavior in the lives of politicians?

Ever since then-presidential-candidate Gary Hart's reported marital infidelity several years ago, sexual immorality has known no rivals as the pinnacle issue in political character-talk. In 1992, the independent candidate for the national presidency, Ross Perot, declared that, if elected, he would not knowingly offer a place in his administration to a person who had committed adultery. According to Perot, marital infidelity disqualifies a person from performing public service with integrity. How?

From a Christian perspective, does an act or a series of acts of sexual infidelity render an individual unfit for effective public service? Please keep in mind that the question is not about moral correctness. Sexual promiscuity and marital infidelity are wrong, bad wrong. However, the question is about political effectiveness, strong leadership within the government. Does sexual wrongdoing in a person's experience override all of that person's strengths for service? Dogmatic answers to character questions come much easier facing the future than looking into the past. As a matter of historical record, several of the nation's most outstanding statesmen have had trouble with monogamous sexual relations. Their political accomplishments for the good of the nation were as unquestionably positive as their sexual antics were undeniably wrong. Do the latter invalidate the former? Should these people's sins have prevented them from ever having an opportunity to become national heroes?

Play a game with time. Suppose documentation proved that Thomas Jefferson, Dwight Eisenhower, and Lyndon Johnson had indulged in sexual misbehavior prior to serving as president of the nation. What if the public were requested to weigh these men's sins against their major contributions to the nation? What role would the character-issue play in judging the presidencies of these individuals? Should the nation have been deprived of the political genius and governmental leadership of Thomas Jefferson because of charges that Jefferson was guilty of sexual indiscretions?

The "Politics of Virtue"

Character concerns rightfully claim a place in political considerations of a candidate's leadership capabilities. But, what is that place? How should voters measure the importance of character issues in relation to the many other issues that ought to be evaluated before casting a vote for a person?

Here are three questions aimed at establishing the importance of character concerns related to a candidate's bid for public office. Though answers to these questions will vary from individual to individual, everyone can benefit from grappling with these inquiries.

(1) *Does a character question about a particular candidate impinge upon that person's abilities related to political decision-making and governmental leadership?* For example, should a person who likes alcoholic beverages be disqualified from a position of political leadership because a voter or a bloc of voters opposes the consumption of alcohol? If the candidate is an active alcoholic who

regularly drinks to a point of emotional confusion and mental disorientation, that's one thing. Such a condition raises serious questions about competence. If the candidate only enjoys an occasional drink, however, that's another matter completely. Though a voter may consider drinking alcoholic beverages wrong, the voter may still prefer the political expertise of a person who drinks to the lack of leadership abilities evidenced in a candidate who abstains from alcohol.

Sometimes voters must ask whether they prefer a politician with impeccable personal morals and little-to-no political expertise over another politician whose private life is morally controversial but whose ability to pass nation-strengthening legislation is unquestionable. An analogy may help clarify the matter. If scheduled for open heart surgery, do you prefer the services of an internationally-acclaimed heart specialist who is a religious agnostic over those of a recent graduate from medical school who is morally orthodox but surgically untested? It's not an easy choice. The path that leads to character judgments about political candidates winds its way through a dangerous mine field.

(2) *What is the relationship between a candidate's private moral character and his/her support for public moral standards?* A person with puritanical moral convictions personally can stand as a roadblock to justice-based legislation socially. Is it better for the nation to be led by people who exhibit exemplary personal spirituality—attending worship services, praying in public, practicing evangelism—whether or not they display a strong conscience regarding social morality—concern for the poor, help for the homeless, food for the malnourished?

More than once an individual with highly questionable personal morals has become a decisive influence in securing the passage of a piece of legislation that strengthened the moral fiber of our nation. Where does judgment about an individual's character fall in such a situation? Of course, we desire a good combination of personal morals and social ethics in our candidates, but we don't always get what we want. Is it more important for an elected official to be concerned about the morals of the nation or to display an attractive personal ethic?

(3) *Does a candidate's potential for public service outweigh the negative impact of his/her past mistakes?* Placed under the powerful

microscope of a media-covered political campaign, few candidates for any office come off looking squeaky clean. Virtually everyone's past contains regrettable errors, mistakes, and sins. Should those past wrongs eliminate the possibility of future leadership? That's the question.

What about the present? Dealing fairly with a person's past requires looking seriously at that person's present. What kind of campaign is the individual running? Does his campaign financing reflect integrity? Is her vision for the nation inclusive of all citizens? Where does he stand on public education, feeding assistance programs for the elderly, and anti-discrimination legislation?

Viewed another way, of what value is a past free from "major" sins for a candidate who wages an electoral campaign filled with slander, mud-slinging, and the language of hatred? How should the boast, "I have never cheated on my spouse," be weighed against the promises, "If elected to office, I will dismantle the whole social welfare system, abolish the federal government's involvement in education, see to it that people pay more for Medicare, and tell other nations that come to us with outstretched hands to take a hike"? Where does the weight of character and morality lie? Past sins do not prevent a person from present service. That is a truth of the Christian gospel as well as a political reality.

Welcome Interest or Dangerous Concern

Public opinion polls document the American people's interest in personal moral behavior. Over three-fourths of the nation's adults worry about a major moral and spiritual decline within the United States.[7] Little wonder a strong emphasis on character is emerging.

At first glance, this enthusiastic interest in character is gratifying. Who can oppose fairness, caring, trustworthiness, and respect? Is that the motivation behind this movement, though? For some, it obviously is. But not for all, not for some of the loudest proponents of character assessments. Could an organized political push to elect candidates of good character—"Virtuecrats"[8]—represent an effort to translate personal moral convictions and principles of a sectarian faith into dictums of social policy?

In the 1950s, ardent religionists launched a major effort to amend the Constitution to make the laws of the nation subservient to the word of God and to the rule of Jesus Christ.[9] In that same tradition, Randall Terry of recent Operation Rescue fame declares that the nation must adopt a legal code based on the Christian religion. "We must have a Christian nation built on God's law, on the Ten Commandments. No apologies," Terry said.[10] Has the prerogative for understanding good character become the sole possession of one group of people?

Character issues fit into the mix of factors conscientious citizens study when preparing to vote for a candidate in an election. Humility rather than self-righteousness greatly aids an assessment of a politician's character, however. There are no more morally perfect candidates for political positions than there are morally perfect citizens to vote for them.

Christians, of all people, view character as important. Yet, grace demands that Christians not deny persons the potential for meaningful service in the future because of immoral actions on their part in their past. Christian citizens, to an extent not expected of other citizens, relate to politicians (as to everyone) with forgiveness—giving individuals who have failed second, third, and fourth opportunities to do better.

Moral Leadership

God knows the nation needs strong moral leadership. But, what constitutes such leadership? What character trait in a politician most beneficially impacts the character of the nation for good?

Edward Tivnan suggests that truly great moral leaders help the nation "reimagine the world we think we know so well, until we realize that something is so wrong with it that we have to create a new world."[11] That's what Abraham Lincoln did for the nation regarding slavery. And, a century later, that was the gift Martin Luther King, Jr. related to racial discrimination. Great moral leaders enable citizens to envision the need for profound changes.

After United States troops returned from Saudi Arabia and their involvement in the Gulf War, Wendell Berry reflected on the meaning of modern warfare. From amid the poet's musings emerged an imaginative agenda for powerful moral leadership. Berry declared,

We must learn to prefer quality over quantity, service over profit, neighborliness over competition, people and other creatures over machines, health over wealth, a democratic prosperity over centralized wealth and power . . . If we want to be at peace, we will have to waste less, spend less, use less, want less, need less.[12]

The nation needs leaders who can help their opponents as well as their supporters recognize a need to cooperate in the cause of moral reform. Such leaders do not exist without strong character. So, yes, a candidate's character is important, terribly important. But the crucial character consideration is not moral perfection in a candidate's personal life (who could ever run for office); rather, a politician's moral vision regarding the character of the nation.

What do a candidate's policy statements promise?

Elections are not popularity contests. Voting for a person means more than affirming that individual or wishing her well. The fate of a government is at stake in every election. And a government is much larger than any one of its officeholders. In the final analysis, the manner in which a government official deals with certain fundamental issues influences the quality of citizens' lives far more than the personality of that official.

A desire for the nation to elect a woman or a minority person to a high office within the government rings true to a concern for social justice. In a national election, however, a candidate's identity as a woman or as a member of a social minority falls short of sufficient justification for voting for that person. Important questions must be answered: What does she stand for politically? What is his motivational vision for the nation? What are her legislative priorities? How does he view the relationship between the federal government and the rights of states? These policy issues equal in importance, if not transcend, a candidate's identity.

In most elections, campaign headquarters make available copies of their candidates' policy statements. These materials provide vital grist for citizens' decision-making mill. Through such documents, voters can learn a candidate's program initiatives, plans for reform, and economic priorities.

Realistically, most people do not devote a large amount of time to extensive reading in a candidate's campaign materials. Every person can choose three or four issues of individual interest and study a candidate's positions on these specific concerns, however. A comparison between our own political platform and the political proposals that various office-seekers discuss during a campaign leads to informed, responsible voting.

Our interests vary, naturally. But, here are a few areas in which knowledge of a candidate's policy proposals can be very significant to a person of faith.

Government

Does the candidate favor a reduction in the size of government? Why? How about cutbacks in government services? What does he advocate that the government do that it is not presently doing, or not do that it now does? Does she view government as a master or a servant?

What is the candidate's philosophy regarding budget issues? Does he favor a balanced-budget regardless of the consequences of achieving that goal? What are her budget priorities? Will he support an increase in taxes? How does she feel about a flat tax rather than an income tax? Would he protect the interests of the poor in economic decision-making?

What responsibilities does the candidate assign to government? Individual values? Religious practices? Family nurture? Economic growth? What areas of life does the candidate consider off-limits for the government?

Social Justice

Is the candidate committed to freedom with justice for all persons? Will she protect individual rights or consider rights a threat to liberty? Does the candidate display sensitivity to the least powerful people in the electorate as well as to high profile individuals of influence?

What is the candidate's position on public education? Does he favor public funding for private schools? Would she abolish the Department of Education?

How does the candidate view affirmative action programs? Is she aware of the problem of reverse discrimination as well as of discrimination? How would he attack the problem of institutional or systemic racism?

Does the candidate favor welfare reform or an abolishment of the welfare system? Will she tap into Social Security funds to get financial support for other services? Does he view Medicare and Medicaid as essential government provisions?

Religious Freedom

Does the candidate prize the principle of religious liberty? Will she insist on government neutrality toward all religions? Does he favor a new amendment to the Constitution to alter the present relationship between religion and government?

How does the candidate view public aid for private education? What role, if any, does she assign to religion within a public school's curriculum? Would he support voluntary student-led prayers in a classroom? What is her position on released-time provisions for religious meetings during a school day?

What issues does the candidate view as religious liberty issues? Will he support the appointment of an ambassador to the Vatican? Does she consider a decision about abortion a matter of religious freedom? Would he want Federal Communications Commission regulations applied to religious broadcasts? Does she support tax exemptions for religious organizations?

International Relations

Is the candidate an isolationist? Or, does he favor the nation's active involvement in the community of nations? What is her understanding of the role of the United States in world politics? Does he support the United States' financial commitment to and political presence in the United Nations?

What is the foundation of the candidate's approach to foreign affairs? Would she hesitate to use military force against an aggressor nation in a part of the world devoid of a United States presence? Does he support the use of the nation's militia as a peace-keeping force in war-torn lands or as a humanitarian force in places where disease and hunger run rampant?

In the candidate's thought, must the United States insist on a democratic form of government among people who receive our foreign aid? Would he support diplomatic relations with nations whose policies our government opposes? Does he consider governments' records on human rights an important factor in deciding whether or not to establish trade agreements with them?

The One-Issue Fallacy

Single-issue voting is dangerous. Generally speaking, no candidate should be supported or opposed on the basis of his views on one subject alone. An official at almost any level of government regularly deals with a host of issues that affect the quality of citizens' lives. Even strong disagreement with a candidate on one area of concern of major interest to us must not blind us to that person's positions on other issues that also will impact our lives and shape our community.

Seldom, if ever, will we find a candidate whose every decision we support. Each voter has to weigh carefully points of agreement and areas of disagreement with a candidate. When an office-seeker's political platform meshes with our own political platforms at numerous key points, we are likely to develop an attraction to that candidate. And, with good reason. If points of agreement never emerge, we best look elsewhere for another candidate to support.

How important is the outcome of an election?

Since faith and politics constitute the focus of this book, an additional word must be added to this discussion about deciding for whom to vote and then voting. Sometimes we make mistakes, occasionally really bad ones. In the course of our political deliberations and actions, we make wrong judgments, err in our evaluations of certain candidates, and cast votes we wish we could recall. That is to be expected. However, God's grace and forgiveness extend into the political realm just as into every other realm of life. We best claim God's gifts.

The outcome of an election is very important. The candidates we elect to office give direction to the government that affects virtually every aspect of our daily lives. A shift in the priorities, provisions, regulations, and financial allocations of a particular office can significantly affect our family's finances, educational involvement, and religious freedom; our personal job security, transportation methods, and attitude toward the future; and society's stability, safety, and liberty. The outcome of an election is very important.

An election is *only* an election, however. Our vote for a specific candidate is just that. We elect political leaders to serve in temporal offices. The votes we cast in a government polling place do not decide the fate of Christianity. A political election cannot alter the sovereignty of God. A proper political position on our part is not a prerequisite to God's reign.

Lest we ever consider an election unimportant, we best study the consequences of past elections. Lest we consider an election too important, though, we best reread a biblical passage tucked away in a very political document known as the book of Revelation. The author of the Apocalypse wrote, "The kingdom of the world has become the kingdom of our Lord and of his Christ, and he shall reign for ever and ever" (Rev 11:15). That eternal truth abides regardless of whether we personally win or lose on a specific civil ballot.

Notes

[1]*The Macon Telegraph*, 19 October 1992, 5A.

[2]All statements in quotations in this section concerning platforms are taken directly from "The Republican Platform 1992" and "The Democratic Party Platform 1992."

[3]Joseph Conn, "Behind the Mask," *Church & State*, November, 1994, 5.

[4]Stephen L. Carter, *The Culture of Disbelief: How American Law and Politics Trivialize Religious Devotion* (New York: Anchor Books, Doubleday, 1994) 98.

[5]Albert J. Menendez, *Religion and the Polls* (Philadelphia: Westminster, 1977) 67.

[6]Ibid., 67, 71.

[7]Howard Fineman, "Virtuecrats," *Newsweek*, 13 June 1994, 31.

[8]Ibid., 32.

[9]Carter, 86.

[10]"America Must Become Christian Nation Under 'God's Law,' Says OR's Terry," *Church & State*, October 1993, 19.

[11]Edward Tivnan, *The Moral Imagination: Confronting The Ethical Issues of Our Day* (New York: Simon & Schuster, 1995) 254.

[12]Wendell Berry, "What We Learned from the Gulf War," *Progressive*, 55, no. 11 (November 1991): 26.

Part IV

FAITH
—*and*—
POLITICS

*Questioning
Our Political Vision*

Notes from a Personal Pilgrimage

On Independence Day, 1979, I delivered a paper on Christian citizenship to the Ethics Commission of the Baptist World Alliance meeting in Brighton, England. I underscored the biblical imperative for responsible citizenship and elaborated individual and institutional implications of this mandate as I understood them. As a period of discussion began at the conclusion of my presentation, a minister from East Germany commented, "I can't identify with any of that." My spirit plummeted. The minister, now my good friend, Christian Wolfe, explained that my conception of a Christian's responsibility for political involvement held virtually no relevance to his situation.

Upon reflection, I knew the East German minister was right. My concept of a Christian's practice of responsible citizenship, like my view of civil government, reflected as much provincial bias as biblical truth.

I left that international meeting on ethics with a resolve to broaden my perspective on the relationship between faith and politics. I had a hunch that other dimensions of my moral vision of government needed expansion as well.

Listening to the World

Blessed by opportunities to travel internationally, I have benefited from listening to Christians whose citizenship must find expression in a variety of governmental contexts. Their worries and words, situations and visions, forced me to reassess the meaning of Christian citizenship.

In Hungary and Romania, prior to the fall of the Berlin Wall, I heard Christians castigate each other. Those who tried to cooperate with government authorities labeled those bent on revolution as "insurrectionists." But the latter fired back, hurling the label of "collaborationists" at the former. Does responsible Christian citizenship require obedience or obstinance in relation to a communist government?

Israeli Christians prodded questions about support for civil authorities who embrace a "holy war" philosophy toward much of the Arab world. Other Christians outside Jerusalem complained about the loss of their homes because of a government-imposed exile from the land of their births.

A minister friend in one of the larger governments of South America anxiously whispered to me about his name's inclusion on a "hit list" of persons to be eliminated at the outbreak of a revolution. In another nation in the southern hemisphere, I spoke with Christians too weak and too poor even to think of political action. A vote meant nothing to these people; a loaf of bread meant everything. Chinese Christians told me wrenching stories of their life under the rule of Mao Tse Tung. I could not identify with the form of citizenship they chose to practice. Neither, though, could I question the fidelity and power of their Christian witness in an incredibly bad situation.

Only recently, in Cuba, I have dialogued with Christian brothers and sisters who cannot understand our government's insensitivity to the needs on their island. They question why Christians support an economic blockade that denies them an opportunity to improve the quality of their lives. The United States government's policy toward Cuba looks very different when sitting on the side of a dirt street in Ciego de Avila, Cuba, eating a crusty piece of bread and worrying about a family member who needs unavailable medication than when dining on a steak and baked potato in Washington, D.C., unconcerned about medical supplies.

A cacophony of voices rings in my head and challenges every word I write about the political vision of Christian citizens. Faith cannot turn a deaf ear to the rest of the world as it charts a course of political action at home.

Changing My Mind

Since my earliest musings on Christian citizenship, I have changed my mind at several points. The source of my beliefs about faith's relationship to politics has not changed. That is not the case, though, when it comes to the certainty with which I apply moral and political principles to people of faith in situations unlike mine. Honest humility has replaced whatever degree of authority formerly buttressed my thoughts about this matter. I agree with Judge Learned Hand who spoke of the "spirit of liberty" as the "spirit that is not too sure it is right."[1]

Presently, I realize that, even in my own nation, I know far more about the Bible's teachings on citizenship than I do about how to be obedient to the Bible's instructions. And now I refuse to tell Christians who live under other forms of government what they should and should not do to honor and express their faith.

One thing I know, unless my political vision as a Christian takes into consideration the whole world with all of its conflicting ideologies, political practices, and massive personal needs, that vision requires expansion.

What's the big deal about political vision?

Vision is important. Without doing exegetical injustice to the biblical text, citing the wisdom of Proverbs (29:18) reinforces a recognition of the significance of vision—"Where there is no vision, the people perish" (KJV). A true application of that divinely-inspired observation extends into the realm of politics.

Christian social critic Jim Wallis believes the United States is, in fact, "perishing" from a lack of "vision,"[2] a word that embraces the concept of "imagination" or "prophetic perspective" (interestingly, translators of the RSV rendered the word "vision" in Proverbs 29:18 as "prophecy"). Devoid of an ability to imagine a new reality, people wallow in the ills and problems of the present. History has always depended upon visionaries to lead people into a better day.

Vision is important, but vision alone is not enough. *What* a person sees is as significant as *that* a person sees. Not just any vision promises health and success for the nation or responsible politics in the life of a person. Politically speaking, the absence of a *correct* vision diminishes the nation and allows individuals' dreams to perish.

A helpful vision connects people to the past as it points to the future. Such a vision, thereby, offers the possibility of transformation in the present. Good visions appreciate good values and initiate high hopes.

A sound political vision among Christians reaches back to the core values of the biblical revelation with a commitment to utilize these values in bringing about growth in the nation. In defining "imagination," Jim Wallis captures the thrust of a Christian's political vision:

[It] means the ability to invent the future, guided by core values, and unrestrained by present ideological assumptions and structural status quo.[3]

Grandiose visions can cripple people and stifle progress. So can visions that are too small. My concern is with visions devoid of breadth. I have no desire to replace longstanding corporate and individual political visions bequeathed to our nation by thoughtful, values-oriented citizens. I do want to expand the parameters of these visions, however, to enlarge what we see, to extend the limits to which we think we can go. Toward that end, I raise three questions about the kinds of expansion needed in the political vision of the nation, of individual citizens, and of Christian citizens in particular.

How does our nation need to expand its political vision?

Self-interest driven actions and a hunger for immediate satisfaction hamper effective politics within our nation and limit our sense of responsibility in the world community. Each of these problems can be corrected by an expanded political vision.

From Me to Us

Earlier I related something of my first foray into politics as a ten-year-old boy on summer vacation. Now, with some embarrassment, let me tell you the rest of that story.

Once the election was over and my candidate had won, I decided to write the new governor a letter offering my congratulations and pledging my continued support (whatever that would mean from a ten-year-old). When I mentioned my intentions aloud, I received advice that altered my sense of personal fulfillment and created a whole new set of political expectations.

Good friends told me that I should let the new governor know how hard I had worked on his behalf and then ask him for a new television set, a new car, or some other sizable expression of his appreciation. I still remember an observation that accompanied one specific suggestion, "That's how it works. That's what politics is all about; there's always a payoff for winners. Ask for yours."

Of course, that sounded good to me. This new information sharpened the edges of my self-interest and whet my appetite for gain even as it reshaped my feelings about the political work I had done. A satisfying sense of service and accomplishment derived from working on behalf of someone else's campaign gave way to excitement about the possibility of a payoff.

My childhood experience provides a parable of political life. "What's in it for me?" serves as a motivational question of great importance to a person making a decision about involvement in political action. The assumption is that if no personal gain is involved, the action in question is not worth the effort. And, most people are looking for a lot more than a new television set or a new car. The hunger is for tax breaks, special considerations in altering regulations, appointment to an office, influence on another politician, or the realization of more power.

Walk around Washington, D.C., and take note of the offices that house various special interest groups. Scan the skyline of the capital city, and you become aware that powerful lobbyists representing labor unions, the National Rifle Association, and other partisan concerns occupy the most imposing buildings facing the offices of our federal officials. Study the daily agenda of a national congressperson, and you will be struck by how much time is spent with people seeking special political favors. Presently, much of the machinery of the federal government runs on fuel supplied by a variety of political pressure groups, each devoted to gaining maximum support for its causes.

Special interest groups are just that—groups interested in special interests; narrow concerns; issues that affect them; policies, privileges, and exemptions that they want. When special interest groups dominate government officials' time and attention, what happens to support for the common good? Who speaks for those who have no lobbyist in Washington? Who represents the best interests of the nation as a whole, the general welfare of the masses over against the narrow concerns of a few?

Christians know well the dangers of a self-centered lifestyle and systems that function on the basis of self-interest. Egoism inflicts harm on politics just as it does spirituality. However, often the political involvements of Christians reflect the same kind of narrow interests that characterize other groups.

A former member of the House Ways and Means Committee decried the flood of Christians that washed over the meeting room of his committee when it was reevaluating the status of charitable contributions as income tax deductions. Actually, he opposed any change, but my friend was put out because these same people were nowhere to be found when his committee reevaluated support for social welfare programs targeted at the neediest people in the land. He saw selfishness, not compassionate social interest, among religious organizations, and it bothered him.

A political process primarily responsive to self-interests will stop short of reaching its full potential as a means of service to humankind. Attending only to the demands of the loud and the powerful blunts sensitivity to the weaker members of society who have no public voice. Additionally, concern for our national interests alone removes us from involvement as a responsible citizen of the world.

The same movement is needed as our nation considers its place in the community of nations. A consideration of the needs of our nation to the exclusion of what is going on in the rest of the world is an invitation to major problems if not disaster. Only as we consider what is best for the world do we set in motion political processes that ultimately will benefit us as well as others. The operative political vision in the nation needs to move from me to us.

From Now to Later

Future generations have no lobbyists. They don't even have a vote. For that reason, the long-range implications of political decisions often do not receive adequate attention by government officials. Politicians settle for efforts to satisfy the most pressing needs of the most prominent pressure groups.

Such a narrow preoccupation with the present represents both political and moral irresponsibility. Permission to carry out ecologically risky methods of exploration for new sources of energy to meet the immediate demands of burgeoning industries may set in motion major environmental problems that will peak at crisis proportions as our grandchildren reach adulthood. Adopting an isolationist posture in relation to the rest of the world to focus on crucial domestic concerns today can exclude our government from the international dialogue so necessary to resolving a growing number of worldwide problems that will directly impact the quality of people's lives tomorrow. Christian citizens have an obligation to speak on behalf of persons who cannot speak for themselves and to see that those who cannot request care still receive care. Thus, Christian citizens serve as advocates for politics as responsible to the future as to the present.

From Independence to Interdependence

Independence is a blessing worthy of constant thanksgiving. The independence of our nation rests on the foundation of visionary ideas written into its formative documents by its founders and costly sacrifices by members of its military forces. Independence has persisted because of vigilance on the part of citizens who understand the precarious nature of freedom and the need for its constant protection. Independence is a blessing.

Interdependence is a reality. A decision by a Senate sub-committee in Washington, D.C., prompts new hopes among the hunger-devastated people of Somalia. Marketing strategies adopted by a meeting of Arab sheiks in the Middle East force a posting of new prices on gas pumps in Charleston, South Carolina. A car bombing in Beirut causes a crisis line to ring in Jerusalem. Trade talks in London incite monetary anxieties in Brussels.

We are not alone on this planet. Neighbors surround us in the community of nations. The plights of our neighbors affect us even as our actions inevitably have repercussions for them. Thanksgiving for independence need not (must not) blind us to the reality and responsibilities of interdependence.

Citizenship in the world is a given. Only the quality of this citizenship remains in question, and answers to that inquiry reside in the specifics of our nation's foreign policies.

Justice issues loom larger all the time. Terrorism, for example, is an international problem, not the concern for one government alone. Effective counter-terrorist strategies necessitate prompt and substantive cooperation between governments not even accustomed to regular communication with each other. International cooperation is also required for the establishment of legal agreements binding on and enforceable in all nations. Multi-national commitments to support a world court make good sense. The United Nations merits major financial contributions and persistent political support. Despite flaws and weaknesses in this world body, the United Nations represents real hope for international dialogue, cooperation, and peace-keeping. Our nation's involvement in the United Nations should leave no doubt in anyone's mind about the strength of our commitment to function as a responsible citizen of the world.

Such talk scares some people. With shrill voices, they warn against the dangers of a monolithic government, a new world order, and a one-world organization that will destroy national freedoms. Actually, Christians recognize the foundation for a vision of interdependence within the prophetic tradition of Old Testament Judaism and support for that vision in the worldwide mission mandated by Jesus Christ and described in the New Testament. God's people have always valued independence while experiencing the joys and accepting the burdens of interdependence.

From a Maintenance of Defense to Initiatives for Peace

Massive, dramatic, revolutionary changes have rocked Eastern Europe. First, the "iron curtain" melted. Then, the Berlin wall tumbled under the assault of freedom-loving people. The monolith of the Soviet Union splintered. Suddenly longtime enemies of the United States looked more like early colonists on the shores of North America trying to establish a viable democracy than dangerous adversaries. Guns and ammunition no longer seemed to provide the basis for a relationship with these people. Attention turned to cooperative economic ventures and viable means of maintaining peace with justice.

Debate continues on the reasons for these massive changes. Some citizens suggest that the dramatic developments in Eastern Europe never would have transpired had the United States not built and maintained an intimidating militia supported by a powerful arsenal of state-of-the-art weapons of destruction. You know the old saying, the best offense is a strong defense. Other citizens counter with a conviction that the sweeping changes would have occurred much earlier had the United States invested in initiatives for peace at the same fiscal level that was devoted to the machinery of war. Agreement between these two points of view is highly unlikely. Thankfully, though, the present challenge requires us to move beyond a debate about the past to develop a strong and impressive unity regarding the necessity of peace work in the present. An altered world situation demands a major change in Americans' attitude about conflict resolution. For many years an expanding budget for national defense, vigorous research and development of new weapons, fool-proof systems for the detection of potential military intrusions, and sensitive surveillance techniques for monitoring other governments occupied the interest of citizens. A defense-oriented, reactionary mindset prevailed.

Today's challenge requires thoughts of peace rather than methods of warfare. A pro-active posture toward conflict resolution inspires creative thoughts about how to meet controversy with discussions rather than threats, with shared opinions rather than intimidation. The nation's strength and will should now be measured by competence in political cooperation rather than military capabilities.

Nay-sayers regarding initiatives for peace possess (or are possessed by) a much too narrow vision. A national commitment to international peacemaking can spur vigorous industrial development and create new jobs. True, the products that bump along assembly lines will be categorically different from tanks, bullets, and bombs; but assembly lines will be running full speed, and Americans will be working. What's more, throughout the nation, people can contemplate the benefits of peace rather than attempt to abide a constant fear that sets life on edge.

How do we need to expand our political vision as individual citizens?

A narrow vision restricts a person's actions. Limited thoughts compromise the possibility of expansive lives. Individual citizens do well to broaden their political vision.

From Freedom to Responsibility

Almost forty years ago, Fulton Sheen, a bishop in the Roman Catholic Church, made an interesting Independence Day proposal. Sheen suggested that the time had come for the nation to erect a Statue of Responsibility on its west coast to complement the Statue of Liberty that stands on its east coast. Whether the suggestion was real or metaphorical, I don't know. Either way the bishop's comment conveyed an essential truth about the relationship between freedom and responsibility. The two go together.

Freedom is tentative at best. Left unwatched and unprotected, freedom can suffer from rapid erosion and even end up ruthlessly destroyed. Freedom requires constant attention—"eternal vigilance," political sages have said. Support for freedom necessitates tireless actions on behalf of freedom. Freedom does not endure for long unless those who enjoy it accept responsibility for its maintenance and live out freedom responsibly.

Negative definitions of freedom don't tell the whole story about freedom. A passive, though grateful, acceptance of the blessings of liberty—guarantees of freedom from a tyrannical government, mandated religion, unjust punishment, and the like—fails to capture the true nature of liberty. Freedom has a positive dimension that finds expression in aggressive actions. Within a democracy, for example, citizens are free *for* responsibility, not free *from* responsibility. In fact, failure to use freedom positively and responsibly creates the possibility of losing freedom completely.

A moral exercise of freedom results in citizenship that strengthens and secures freedom for all persons. Freedom from bondage frees a person to work for the elimination of all forms of oppression. Freedom from taxation without representation frees citizens to support an equitable system of taxation and a just usage of government funds collected through taxes.

Take a look at the constitutional guarantee of religious freedom. Church-state separation defines the negative dimension of this fundamental liberty. We are free from a church-run state or a state-run church, free from taxation based on religious persuasion, free from coercion regarding religious convictions, free from punishment for practicing religion or rejecting religion. That is only a partial picture of the nature of religious liberty, however. Religious freedom has a positive dimension. Under the provisions of the First Amendment, we are free to worship, free to share our faith, free to speak prophetically to society, free to exert our influence in government, and free to do none of this if we so choose. Where freedom prevails, what we consider ourselves free *for* is every bit as important, if not more so, as what we consider ourselves free *from*. A citizen's political vision should always be broad enough to embrace responsibility.

From Voting to Politicking

Voting is to democracy what a heartbeat is to a human's body. Participation in the electoral process is so vital to the health of a democracy, in fact, that I am almost persuaded every citizen should be required by law to vote (a policy extant in many governments). By casting ballots for candidates for public office, citizens exercise the right to choose their political leaders. Knowing that ballots will be cast, political leaders try to be responsive to citizens.

Voting is important. Voting rightfully occupies a place of centrality in responsible citizenship. However, an individual's political vision is far too narrow if voting in an election suffices as a substitute for engaging in political action. Sequentially, voting occurs way down the road in politics. At a polling place, people only have an opportunity to react to decisions already made. Long before election day, precinct meetings and local caucuses choose which candidates will represent the major political parties and independent interests in an election. Only through regular participation in base political organizations do citizens have an opportunity to shape ballots as well as to cast votes.

Voting represents the best of democracy. Realistically, though, democracy could not continue if citizens did no more than vote. In the lives of conscientious citizens, voting is one political activity among many. Other important responsibilities include support for a political party, interaction with local government officials, regular correspondence with congresspeople, advocacy for public education, and membership in special interests groups—to name a few.

Shaping public opinion is political action of the highest order. Abraham Lincoln considered the molding of public opinion a more important act than passing legislation. The former president explained that a person who influences public opinion helps determine whether or not executive pronouncements and legislative enactments can be enforced. Thankfully, every citizen can (and should) be involved in politics at this point—speaking intelligently and persuasively about personal convictions, writing letters to government leaders, using the local media to communicate a point of view, calling for special studies in religious bodies and civic organizations.

In a democracy, all citizens bear the identity of politicians, like it or not. Obviously, some do a good job, and some hardly function at all. Some citizens exercise great political influence among their circle of acquaintances, while others contribute little to anyone else's thoughts.

An individual's political vision needs to contain a voting booth, to be sure. In that vision, however, the voting booth should set in a context of multi-faceted political activities.

From Declared Promises to Enacted Policies

American politicians throw around promises like parade-goers toss confetti. Unlike confetti that falls harmlessly to the ground, though, politician's promises work on people's minds. Voters love promises, and they respond positively to promise-makers. So, politicians continue their wholesale distribution of one promise after another—"I'll lower taxes, cut the unemployment rate in half, balance the budget, raise the minimum wage, improve roads . . ."

When the public follows the example of its political leaders, rhetoric becomes the most popular form of political action. People talk good government despite an absence of actions to support their conversations. Most political positioning in the United States comes by talking.

Talk is good. Political conversations serve a useful function, but stirring oral declarations are no substitute for meaningful political actions. In politics as in religion, both words and deeds are required to reach goals and fulfill promises. The real test of an individual's political will resides in substantive actions—not in what a person promises to do but in what a person attempts to get done.

An official's promise to downsize government requires support for specific programmatic reductions, some of which may take away benefits enjoyed by the reformer. A politician's pledge to bring honesty to government may necessitate admitting publicly, "I made a bad decision; my support for the redistricting legislation was wrong," even when that confession could cost her re-election. A citizen's resolve to live as a peacemaker necessitates accepting the difficulties involved in vocational retooling as a weapons industry transforms itself into a manufacturer of domestic products. Discussions of our vision for the nation should occur at every opportunity. However, to make a real difference in the nation we discuss, actions must complement talk—actions such as organizing a coalition to support a piece of legislation, participating in a voter registration drive, drafting a sample piece of legislation, speaking to the city council, chairing a neighborhood forum, and functioning in precinct politics.

As a person's political vision continues to expand, specific, detailed forms of personal political action give substance and strength to that vision. Promises are good for the public's psyche. Fulfilled promises actually alter the nature and course of government.

As Christian citizens, how do we need to broaden our political vision?

The content of a healthy political vision is the same for Christians as for non-Christians. All that I have written about a broadened perspective for the nation and for individual citizens applies to Christians. In addition, at least two other concerns merit thought-expanding attention from Christians.

From a "Christian America" to a "Free America"

"Christian America" is a serious misnomer. The concept of a Christian nation persists as a theological heresy and a political impossibility. Biblically speaking, only the church can approximate expectations associated with the idea of a Christian nation—a community of people under the lordship of Christ who serve as priests to each other. Citizenship in the nation differs substantially from citizenship under the rule of God, however.

Attempts to Christianize a government run two major risks. A serious look at the possible consequences of a government-endorsed faith may help nudge Christians toward a broader political vision.

Jeopardizing Freedom. Religiously zealous and personally sincere though they may be, individuals interested in Christianizing America suffer from a dangerously narrow vision—narrow whether measured religiously or politically. Working to establish a national faith jeopardizes everyone's freedom to practice a personal faith. Once a law permits the elevation of one religion above others on the basis of a majority vote, a majority of citizens can negate that very religion by the same method.

Perhaps, at the present moment, a majority of United States citizens would vote to endorse Christianity as the nation's official religion. But think what such a judgment would do to persons who confess a different faith or no faith at all. Their status as a minority would threaten their liberty. Then again, consider the fate of Christians once a majority of the citizenry endorsed a faith other than Christianity.

The same constitutional provision that prevents a Baptist child from Mormon indoctrination in the public schools of Salt Lake City, Utah, also prevents a Muslim child from Christian indoctrination in Memphis, Tennessee. Give up one and the other goes with it. The law that prohibits a Christian-oriented government from devoting tax money to support Christian schools can prevent an Islamic president of the United States from designating public funds to erect mosques and minarets in every municipality of the union. Remove that law and the religion that prevails in the White House or on Capitol Hill can be enforced as the preferable religion of the nation.

But isn't that a far-fetched possibility, a hypothetical scare tactic? Does anyone harbor a vision so narrow? Judge for yourself.

In 1991, the President of the African nation of Zambia, Frederick Chiluba, declared his country "a Christian nation." In the spring of 1995, Chiluba appeared as a guest on Pat Robertson's television show called the "700 Club." While contending that he intended tolerance toward other religions, the Zambian president explained that, over the protests of other religions, he declared his nation "Christian" so people would have a "yardstick" by which to judge it.

Television host Robertson, who leads the powerful Christian Coalition, responded to Chiluba with a chilling comment. "Your country," Robertson said, "is a standard for not only Africa but the rest of the world." Turning to his audience, Robertson asked, "Wouldn't you love to have someone like that as President of the United States of America?"[4]

Robertson's endorsement of a Christianization of the nation is not without support. A reconstructionist-minded candidate for Congress in the state of Georgia in 1986, Joseph Morehead, on separate occasions declared, "Jesus Christ is the unrivaled monarch of the political process of the United States of America," and "the only hope for the United States is the total Christianization of the country at all levels."[5]

Committed to a similar philosophy, though working only at the level of state government, Jay Grimstead, leader of the Coalition on Revival, stated in a 1990 interview, "It is the goal of a number of us to Christianize the state of California."[6] A more mainline Religious Right leader, Paul Weyrich, described his work, saying, "We are talking about Christianizing America."[7]

Attempts to identify the nation with one religion makes government subservient to one faith and jeopardizes freedom.

Trivializing Faith. When religion links up with government (or attempts to) in any official manner, religion loses its credibility. Persons who try to use the government to proselytize adherents to their faith usually end up getting used by the government and seeing their faith trivialized.

To attach the adjective "Christian" to partisan political views trivializes Christian convictions. One cannot speak of a Christian health care plan, a Christian platform on economic reform, or a Christian balanced budget amendment in the same manner as referring to Christian truth or Christian doctrine.

Numerous court decisions in this country document a trivialization of faith brought about by some Christians' insistence that government property and funds be used in the perpetuation of a sectarian faith. In what has come to be known as "the plastic reindeer rule," the Supreme Court ruled that using tax money to fund the display of a manger scene on public property at Christmas was constitutionally acceptable. But, get the reason why. The court found the nativity scene in question acceptable because it was surrounded by all kinds of secular Christmas symbols such as candy canes, trees, and reindeer. Writing the majority opinion on this case, Chief Justice Warren Burger indicated no concern for a strict separation between church and state but an accommodation between the two.[8] Subsequent court actions have considered reproductions of the Bethlehem birth scene not so much a religious symbol as a cultural adornment to the season akin to Santa and his sleigh.

As a Christian, I find that judicial ruling totally abhorrent. To liken a depiction of the birth of Christ to a holiday decoration offends me. I cannot understand linking the Incarnation of Almighty God with a reference to Santa Claus and his reindeer. That is a ghastly, sacrilegious, trivialization of the Christian faith!

A few years ago, in a neighboring town, a citizen challenged the legality of the municipality's official seal because the word "Christian" was imprinted on it. Defending the insignia against its challenger via a radio interview, a political leader in that city said he considered "Christianity" a "patriotic" word with "no theological or religious significance."

What Christians lose far exceeds what Christians gain when trying to Christianize the government and thereby use the government to Christianize the nation. We do not need the government to do the work of the church. We only need the government to guarantee a religious freedom that allows the church to do its work alongside the work of other groups.

Citizens who cannot politically support freedom for people of all faiths cannot realistically expect a continuation of freedom for the practice of their faith. Christians with an enlarged political vision readily see and appreciate an endangered freedom.

Politicizing (Desacralizing) Religion. Religious institutions that become preoccupied with political concerns lose their prophetic voice and take on the identity of just another political action group. Religious leaders begin to compete and conflict with each other like the politicians with whom they align themselves. When an interest in political correctness supersedes a commitment to faith, religion evidences "a language and practice that seem more bureaucratic and ideological than spiritual."[9] Both government and religion lose when this happens. The nation is deprived of the unique gifts that come from authentic religious resources.

Jim Wallis charges that the two major forms of contemporary religion in the United States have failed to provide the kind of spiritual guidance that gives politics a conscience and informs it with moral values. Wallis wrote, "Both conservative and liberal religion have become culturally captive forces that merely cheer on the ideological camps with which each has identified." Wallis concluded, "Religion as a political cheerleader is invariably false religion."[10]

Religious institutions best serve people and relate to government by functioning as religious institutions. When immersed in politics, religious institutions leave "the ground of a genuinely independent and prophetic political witness largely unexplored."[11] A comment from William Ernest Hocking merits memorization:

> It is only religion reaching the ultimate solitude of the soul that can create the unpurchasable man, and it is only man unpurchasable by any society that creates the sound society.[12]

From Victory to Fidelity

Politics thrives on winning elections, passing legislation, and amassing power. Significantly different, Christianity finds its clearest expression through humility, servanthood, and integrity. Fully aware of the conflicting natures of politics and Christianity, Christians enter the political realm with a set of goals that differs dramatically from that of many of their colleagues. A Christian is convinced that the ultimate judgment on political activity resides within the providence of God rather than with the whims of the nation or the votes of its citizens. Spiritual fidelity cannot be decided by a vote.

The Theory. Christians properly target success as a goal when working in politics. However, political victory is *a* goal, but not *the* ultimate goal for Christian citizens. The aim of Christian service can be summed up in the word "fidelity"—fidelity in acting for the good of other people and fidelity in acting for the glory of God.

Christian politicians enjoy a permission and a dimension of freedom not known by all people in government. It's alright to lose. Faced by a choice between making a decision that will compromise the truth but assure winning an election and maintaining personal integrity, Christians opt for integrity. In such a situation, the next day's newspaper may label the Christian politician a loser. The description is accurate from the perspective of counted votes; the election was lost. But neither voters nor journalists really pronounce the final judgment on such a matter. To lose politically in order to remain faithful to spiritual integrity is to win.

The Reality. For sixteen years, Brooks Hays served as a member of the United States House of Representatives. After that tenure, this active Baptist layman counseled United States presidents. Brooks, my dear friend, learned firsthand how fidelity to what is right can result in political victory for what is wrong.

In 1958, Brooks Hays failed in his bid to win another term in the United States Congress. Arkansas voters in the district Brooks served elected a write-in candidate who was an ardent segregationist. Probably the death knell for Brooks' congressional career rang a year earlier when he served as a go-between for President Eisenhower and Governor Faubus of Arkansas in an effort to desegregate the public schools of Little Rock in a peaceable manner.

On numerous occasions I have listened to Brooks reminisce about coming downstairs to breakfast the morning after the election. His wife Marion, whom he fondly called "the little general," asked how he was doing. Brooks indicated that he was upset because he couldn't have his favorite cereal for breakfast. Wheaties, the "breakfast of champions," was his cereal of choice. Marion quickly instructed Brooks to eat his Wheaties, letting him know that in her mind he was still a winner. He was a winner in the minds of many other people too.

Hounded by hostile segregationists who opposed what their incumbent representative to Washington stood for, Brooks Hays lost a crucial political vote. It cost him his seat in Congress, but Brooks Hays retained his personal integrity and demonstrated many of the most basic values in Christian morality.

Not long after that election, 700 people gathered at a dinner to honor Brooks and Marion Hays. To the surprise of almost all in attendance, neither of the Hays shed a tear in the course of a very emotional evening. Others wept openly. Senator John Sherman Cooper from Kentucky was one of them.

A year after that special evening, during a conversation with Senator Cooper, Brooks asked him about his emotions that evening and gently chided him for weeping. Senator Cooper explained his tears in total seriousness, "I was not weeping for you, Brooks; I was weeping for my nation."

In a political situation where integrity is on the side of a loser, tears are in order. When achieving a political victory within government necessitates acts of infidelity in relation to a person's faith, winning is not worth it. Under such circumstances, to lose is to win.

Christian citizens function most responsibly with a political vision broad enough to value freedom that allows diversity more than forced unity and to claim the freedom to lose a political skirmish when winning means forfeiting spiritual faith and personal integrity.

Notes

[1]Learned Hand, "The Spirit of Liberty," *The Spirit of Liberty* (New York: Alfred A. Knopf, 1952) 190.

[2]Jim Wallis, *The Soul of Politics: A Practical and Prophetic Vision for Change* (New York: The New Press and Orbis Books, 1994) 41.

[3]Ibid., 220.

[4]" 'Christian Zambia' is Model for United States, Robertson Insists," *Church & State*, June 1995, 19.

[5]David Cantor, *The Religious Right: The Assault on Tolerance & Pluralism in America* (New York: Anti-Defamation League, 1994) 97.

[6]Ibid., 129.

[7]Ibid., 91.

[8]Ronald B. Flowers, *That Godless Court? Supreme Court Decisions on Church-State Relationships* (Louisville KY: Westminster/John Knox Press, 1994) 123. See also 123-125 for a discussion of another case involving displays of a Christian nativity scene and a Jewish menora.

[9]Wallis, 37.

[10]Ibid., 36.

[11]Ibid., 37.

[12]William Ernest Hocking, cited in Bill Moyers, "On Being a Baptist," *Religion & Values in Public Life: A Forum from Harvard Divinity School*, 1:3 (Spring 1993): 2.